Goodbye, Again

Goodbye, Again

Essays, Reflections, and Illustrations

Jonny Sun

HARPER PERENNIAL

NEW YORK • LONDON • TORONTO • SYDNEY • NEW DELHI • AUCKLAND

HARPER ● PERENNIAL

HarperCollins books may be purchased for educational, business, or sales promotional use. For information, please email the Special Markets Department at SPsales@harpercollins.com.

FIRST EDITION

Designed by Jamie Lynn Kerner

Library of Congress Cataloging-in-Publication Data has been applied for.

ISBN 978-0-06-288085-7

21 22 23 24 25   LSC   10 9 8 7 6 5 4 3 2 1

*For my parents, who I have said goodbye to
more than anyone else, which I suppose is
in itself its own kind of blessing.*

FOREWORD: *A little hello*

2018 was supposed to be the year where I actively got more rest. I had felt burned out from the relentlessness of the world, and from my attempts to retreat into "productiveness"—to spend all my time focused on something that I knew would bring me stress but in exchange would give me some semblance or Illusion of control—in the hopes that I could find some solace in the distractions of always having something I should be working on. All of that led to even deeper burnouts, which led to deeper depressive episodes, which ultimately led to a bargain I made with myself that said I needed to start taking better care of myself if I were to continue to survive. And so 2018 was supposed to be the year where I actively did that. And for a while, I was doing well. I was learning to take breaks and to get rest—not the type of rest that actually just builds more pressure because you feel like you are putting off something you should be doing, but actual, true, healing rest.

Then, between quiet moments, I started squirreling away

thoughts that I made sure to write down so I wouldn't forget them, collecting ideas and little drawings, hoarding them.

I set out trying to be less trapped by the pressure to be constantly productive, and as soon as I started finding those moments where I allowed myself to stop working or thinking about working for a second, to find ways to relax, to recover, to let my mind meander for the sake of it, I decided that I needed to write about them, that I had to document them and collect them or else I would forget them and lose them. Otherwise, I told myself, all this break-taking, this intentionally unproductive time, would not be "worth it."

Somewhere, that desire to have some sort of *proof* that I was taking time off turned into the idea that this needed to be a project, that my time spent not being "productive" had to have a product in order to be worth doing.

This morphed into the thought that I couldn't let this writing *just* be for myself. There was this constant voice in my head telling me that my own rest and recovery and catharsis were not valuable to anybody (or perhaps more honestly, I thought they were not valuable to myself) unless I could have something to show for it, unless I could share it. Otherwise, I was just being selfish for taking a break, for trying to heal or grow in private. That pressure—that I needed something to show for my time—tied to how deeply engrained I am in our culture of constant work and demand and production and optimization—felt inescapable. I felt—and still feel—trapped inside of it.

So, instead of taking a break where I could find a little bit of rest, I looked forward to "break time" because it let me work on something else.

From this break-taking, these essays came. A year of trying to take a break became two years, then three years, of writing and putting these pieces together and working on this book. And over those three years, working on this book kept me some consistent sort of company as I navigated some destabilizing goodbyes, of moving out of different rooms and different apartments and leaving different cities, and then some destabilizing hellos, of trying to find ways to live in the new places I landed in.

Writing through all of this allowed me some stable way to focus on some feelings, to figure out some of my unspoken habits, and to articulate some things that were important to me. So now, I can hold these things in my hand and I can refer to them in the future, a collection of Things I Figured Out or Things I Care About. And that feels like growth, or progress. Or maybe I'm just trying to justify that I find more comfort in work than in rest. Maybe it's a little bit of both.

These essays are short as an acknowledgment that we are all burned out and don't have enough time as it is, so I am just stealing a moment or two from you, whenever I am able to, in the same way I have been stealing moments away—stealing little breaks and stealing from little breaks—to write this. I don't want to burden you or ask for much, and I hope you can visit these as you steal moments away for yourself whenever you can, and I hope they offer something to you, and I hope that's enough, and I hope that's all right.

Goodbye, Again

Part 1: Goodbye

Moving

Every time I move, my guitar is the last thing I pack. After I move out all the boxes, all the moving supplies, all the furniture, I set aside about thirty minutes to play some songs in my home, or what was my home for so long, now empty. I allow my voice to fill up all its rooms for the last time, in the exact way I choose it to, in the exact way I'd like my voice to be remembered here, and the exact way I'd like to remember it here, too. After so many moves, I've learned that this is how I enjoy saying goodbye to a room the most.

This time, I am in my now-empty basement-level (sorry, *Garden-Level*—as the listing so persuasively described it) apartment.

A couple nights ago, I moved my bed to disassemble its frame and in doing so, I revealed a corner that I had never really looked at before. There was a power outlet there, right behind my head, that I never knew existed. I must have overlooked it when I put my bed in this spot when I first moved in—or maybe, more realistically, I had noticed it when I got here but then forgot about it in the general chaos of trying to fill the empty space.

Knowing this power outlet existed right by my head where I slept would have been helpful. I'd been charging my phone from a power outlet by the doorway, far enough away from my bed that if I were already in bed and on my phone at night, I would have to get out of bed and walk over to the power outlet to plug in my phone, and then get back into bed, but now without my phone. And this led to a lot of late nights staying awake on my phone because I didn't want to get out of bed to plug in my phone, but I also didn't want to go to sleep without charging it, and so I just did what any sensible person would do, what felt like the compromise, which was to stay on my phone in bed until my phone died, at which point I would get out of bed to charge it because I could no longer be on it. I wanted to get a longer charging cord or an extension cable, but I had never gotten around to it in the two years I had lived here.

In this one move of revealing a power outlet that would have saved me so many hours of lost sleep, suddenly this place was strange again, just as strange to me as the first time I saw it, empty and new, when I moved in. I thought by living here, I knew everything about this space. I leave it wishing I'd paid more attention to it.

I spent my last night and my first night here sleeping on a mattress on the floor surrounded by boxes. A bed frame was constructed then deconstructed in the time in between. Living in a place feels like it's bookended by parallel experiences. You move into an empty space feeling uncertain about it, and slowly, you let the space hold onto that uncertainty so you don't have to. And when you leave, you leave it again as an empty space, taking back the uncertainty that you were storing in it. It ends with an empty room, the same way as it began, although you've changed in all the time in between. (In my case, the biggest tangible change seemed to be that in my last night here, I plugged my phone into this newly discovered power outlet for the very first time, and I got a slightly better night of sleep than I've had in perhaps the last two years.)

Now, in the morning after, in the last morning that I live here, after I have moved out the mattress and all the boxes and the phone charger, now that all of my belongings and my uncertainties no longer have this place to call their home, it feels like there's nowhere left for dust to hide. There's nothing left to hide the cracks along the walls, the spots of chipped paint that cover up some quick repair work that don't quite exactly match the original color of the room, the gaps where the floor pulls down and away from the baseboard to reveal where the air and the bugs can get in. There's nothing to hide that the light outside doesn't *really* reach the back of this north-facing basement-level—sorry, *Garden-Level*—apartment. Is it colder now, with all my stuff, all that insulation, gone, too? Or am I imagining that? The windows—squat and small, positioned at my eye level, which is just above where the asphalt from the parking lot outside meets the wall of my unit—are single-paned and framed with wood so that they leak around the edges whenever the snow piled up on the ground outside in the winter, or when it rained too hard over the rest of the year. It was always cold, I suppose.

Everything echoes here now in this new hollowness. There is nothing left to absorb the sound, and nothing left to absorb me either. Now I'm not part of the space; I just bounce off the walls, echoing until I leave.

As I play my guitar here, I jump around from song to song, relishing how these songs I know by heart sound in this new, rare echoing. I've played these songs many times in this room, but it had always been with my stuff around. Now, they sound fuller, louder, almost freer. And I am giving one last chance for the room to hear them, and to hear me, before I go.

I hate ending songs when I play, which once made me a terrible performer, before I stopped performing at all. Songs with great, beautiful, perfect endings feel too sad for me to play all the way through. I can't face that ending, that feeling of finality, that no more of the song comes after it (even a song that fades out slowly, as if to suggest that its chorus continues looping forever and ever and it's just that you are growing more and more distant from it, ends with silence), so I play each song I know about halfway through, I stop mid-word, switch over to the beginning of another one, then I get as far as the bridge in that next one before I have this voice in my head that suddenly goes, *All right, that's enough*. Then whatever chord I played last, mid-phrase, before this thought entered my head, hangs in the air for a second, then disappears. And then, that's it here. That's enough.

I suppose that all I hope for is for this home to remember me the way I remember it: imperfect, quiet, creaking, but always trying to be something better than it is on paper, in person, in memory. And I hope for neither of us to see each other again, lest it breaks the spell.

Visiting

You can't outrun sadness because sadness is already everywhere.
Sadness isn't the visitor, you are.

Filling the blankness

There is a specific type of emptiness in moving to a new place to start a new job or start at a new school and not having a life figured out there yet and not really knowing anyone there yet and being faced with the blank-slate openness of Saturday and Sunday and realizing you're just trying to make it through the weekend to get back to having Some Defined Purpose again on Monday.

This blankness is one of the scariest things to me. I don't enjoy having time that's been unaccounted for because it immediately makes me feel like I should be *doing something* with it, and then I can't think of anything that I could possibly be doing that would be worthwhile enough to live up to the raw potential of any amount of available time. Nothing I choose to fill that time with feels like it would be enough. And it makes me sad that the thing that feels closest is taking any time and converting that into some sort of productiveness. I think instead of turning to people, or to hobbies, or to Going Places, or Seeing Things, I find it easiest to turn to doing more work to try to fill, or perhaps keep at bay, that emptiness and that feeling that I can't ever fill that emptiness enough.

In the same way that sadness is always there, I find the idea of work, and working, comforting. It feels like I can leave everything else behind, but as long as I am with myself, I can always work, I can always do *something* with my time. It is something I can always turn to.

This is a learned response. *People will forgive you for not doing anything else with your time or for not having any free time at all if you're busy,* I tell myself. *People will praise you for working more, for finding more time to be productive.* Every time I do this, I reinforce this attitude and this lie that work is more important than anything else, and I fall deeper and deeper for it.

So, on my Saturdays and Sundays, instead of going outside, instead of exploring the city, instead of trying to make friends with the few people I only barely know here, instead of having a weekend, I make up another project for myself, I hole myself up and work and write and catch up on other projects, and fill up all the emptiness until I can have a purpose and a fullness defined for me again on Monday.

Succulent

Never overwater a succulent to try to get it to grow faster. It will not grow faster. You will drown its roots and the roots will rot and then the plant will die.

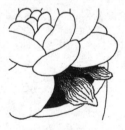

As the older outer leaves grow and get further from the center of the plant, let them dry out and fall away when they are ready to. Do not worry about them. It is natural for what is away from the center of the plant to fall away. It is part of how the plant allocates its resources to survive.

With time, new leaves will grow. When they do, they will grow from the center. It will be slow, but if you take time to notice them, every new day will reveal a tiny bit of growth, and over time, that growth will become apparent.

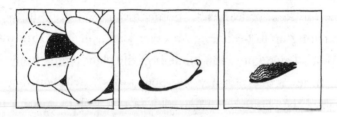

To propagate the succulent, you can try to separate one of the healthy leaves at its base, bending it until it separates where it joins the stem, and then setting it out to dry. I have been told that, sometimes, with enough time and the right conditions, this separated leaf might scab over and grow roots at its base, which you can place in soil, and which, with luck, will grow into a new succulent. I have never gotten this to work. It always feels like I kill the leaf by removing it when it wasn't meant to be removed. The leaves I separate this way always dry out.

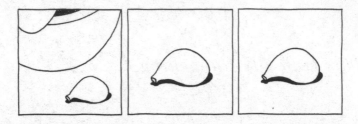

Sometimes, though, a leaf that is still plump and healthy will not need any external force. It will naturally fall off the plant, seemingly ahead of its time, still green and healthy and not at all dried up and moved away from the center just yet. You can place this kind of leaf aside. Sometimes it will dry out, too, as if catching up to becoming an outer leaf, as if it had meant to do that all along but it had fallen off the plant prematurely. But sometimes, it does not dry out. Sometimes, it tells you that it is meant to be planted in a new pot, in new soil, to create a new plant. Sometimes, when something falls away naturally, it forms roots of its own.

This Is Really Happening

I've found that acknowledging good things as Really Happening usually sends me into deep spirals of doubt and anxiety and so I've learned to float through most good things without acknowledging that they're real or happening at all.

A friend asked me, after an Objectively Good And Exciting Thing happened, if I celebrated it. I laughed it off with a "Ha! no," which I still feel bad about. I didn't mean to make my friend feel like it was a dumb question. It's just that I've made the concept of celebrating anything such a foreign thing to me because if I do, that means it's happening, and if it's happening that means I can severely screw it up, and if I severely screw it up that means it will not be happening anymore, and if it is not happening anymore that means that everyone will know that I severely screwed it up, and this all causes me to get so anxious that I feel more likely and more able to screw the thing up than I did before, and so I've found that in general it's just easier to just ignore it and just try to get through it without imagining and then willing into existence all the ways I can go about messing it up.

This prevents me from becoming totally frozen with anxiety, but it also means that I can never really truly enjoy that good things are happening, or even fully be aware that they are happening to begin with.

Another part of my fear of celebrating something as Really Happening is the fear that celebrating it will make me unable to be critical about it, which I fear will make me unable to do a good job at it. I have been trying to tell myself that I can have joy for something and still be critical of it, it's just that I'll become attentive out of love, instead of being critical out of fear, or out of anxiety, or out of some illusion of objective detachment, right?

When you truly fall in love with something, aren't you even more attentive and detailed toward it? After all, not everything out in the world is something you love, right? Loving something is very specific, nuanced. If the cynical approach asks, "What can I do to make this something I don't hate?" perhaps a joyful approach can come from asking, "What am I doing that makes this something I genuinely love?"

I try for the joyful approach, but—you know—loving something is one of those things that is hard to acknowledge as Really Happening, too.

"What about your guilt is helping you?"

I have taught myself to feel like I am constantly failing everyone around me because it pushes me to get things done. I know it's not healthy, but it works because when I make myself feel like I'm letting everyone down all the time, and when I feel like I am always disappointing everyone, then I don't want to disappoint them more, and so I try to work harder to make them less disappointed in me.

This feels . . . productive, I suppose? And when I build up enough of this guilt, I use the focused amounts of it as a compass to tell myself what I *should* be working on at any given moment based on what I can't help but feel guilty about.

When my therapist asks me, "Is this guilt necessary?" I say, "Oh, absolutely. I wouldn't get anything done without it."

And then when he asks, "But what about joy? Can you make joy necessary?"

I pause, then say, "Well, I guess I feel a little relief from building up the guilt and then absolving it by getting things done."

When I reach for an approach that incorporates joy, this is the closest I've come.

On yearning

The most productive years of my life so far have also been my loneliest. I don't know if the loneliness was a requisite for this, but I also don't have any productive years where I haven't been lonely to compare this to. Even knowing that "most productive" should not be the goal of my years to begin with, I have still learned to be more comfortable with being isolated than with being unproductive.

When I am not able to work—when I am out with friends, or having a conversation with someone, or traveling, or buying groceries, or doing the laundry, or eating—I get this itchy, hollow longing that doesn't go away until I am in front of my work again.

If I were talking about a person, I suppose that might be called love.

It doesn't feel right to call this feeling by the same name.

Unnatural words

I have tried to become more attentive to words that treat natural elements of ourselves as currency: "*paying* attention," "*spending* time," "*wasting* energy."

I have tried to catch myself whenever I use words and phrases like this, and when I do, I try to use other words—"*giving* my attention," "*sharing* my time," "*using* my energy"—but I have to go against this immediate, split-second resistance to using words that do not promise that I get something in return for "spending" myself on something. Even though I don't want to feel this way, even though I know this is a reaction learned from a culture of work and production and commodification, it still gives me a brief gut reaction of feeling ripped off, I guess, to talk about giving myself away without any promise of getting anything back.

This language contributes to a belief that we are nothing more than human-shaped machines mining our natural resources for value, but in some terrible trick, it also, somehow, comforts me to know that I have all sorts of currencies that naturally come from me that I can spend. And I hate that this is comforting in a way that simply knowing I have myself to give and to share is not.

Cactus

When I was in Grade 9, I decided I wanted to own a cactus—not just any cactus, but this particularly plump, round cactus that I saw in the area near the entrance of the grocery store where they sell plants sometimes. I had never wanted a cactus before, but this one made me feel really happy when I looked at it, and I asked my parents to buy it for me, and they asked if I would take care of it, and I promised that I would, so I got to bring it home, and I kept it on the nightstand by my bed. I watered it every month or so, or whenever my parents said I should, and I loved it. It made me happy.

When the cactus got infested with little mites, or maybe little spiders, I became inconsolable. I thought it was dying and that nothing could save it. My parents said they would take care of it, and gently moved it out of my bedroom and kept it in their bedroom. Soon after, I forgot about it. My parents never brought it up and so I assumed it had died. Years later, when I moved out, I left without a single thought of that cactus in my mind.

Recently, when I was visiting my parents, I was out with

them and my brother and we walked past a plant shop that we had passed by hundreds of times when I was younger, and I decided to go in for the first time because I wanted to buy my brother a plant. My brother protested with a "Why!"—he doesn't own any plants, at least not yet, so he doesn't know why anyone would own a plant, and I said wistfully, "Remember that cactus I used to have?" And my dad said, "We still have it."

When we got back home later, he showed it to me. At some point after I had moved away, my parents had moved the cactus into the living room, hidden behind a desk, facing a window. After all these years, it had grown tall and crooked. It reached vaguely diagonally, in the direction of the nearest window, and its base had shriveled and dried up and turned woody while the new growth up top stayed wide and green and so it appeared to bulge from its hardened base, plump and round, as if the original plump round ball it started off as was lifting itself up higher and higher, attempting to offer itself to the light.

I was surprised—first because I thought that a round cactus would have just grown into a bigger round cactus instead of this warped, lopsided column, but then second because it was still alive at all.

I felt guilty for forgetting about it, then felt guilty that my parents had taken care of this thing I had so easily forgotten about. Then, this guilt gave way to a flooding of this feeling of appreciation for them, and for their attention (which I then felt guilty about for not feeling sooner). In looking at this tall, crooked column, I was looking at ten years of my parents taking care of this plant that was once so important to me, that I thought had died, that I had moved on from, and that my parents had healed from its mites, or maybe its spiders, and had kept alive all this time.

In seeing my cactus like this, I realized, for what felt like the first time, that my parents kept plants in their home—I knew, objectively, that I'd grown up with plants around me, and I remember plants being around in every memory I have of visiting my parents, but it felt like I had never truly seen them until this moment, standing in my parents' home. . . .

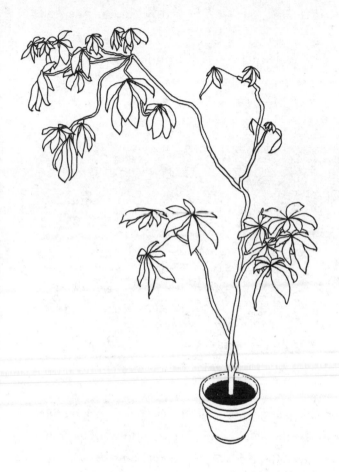

A gangly, overgrown money tree crowds its corner, its un-kempt head of leaves and branches bending against the ceiling as if it is disappointed that it had grown tall enough to reach it, and could never grow any taller.

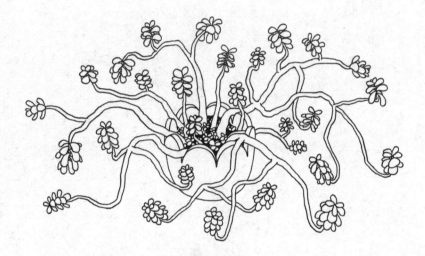

A large old jade plant, whose pot sits in a plastic bag on top of a bin of papers by the window, doesn't seem to want to grow upward at all but instead spreads all its woody branches out, covering a surprisingly wide reach, trying to lay claim over the entire space above the floor between the couch and the TV.

. . . When I had first seen my cactus in the grocery store and brought it home, I remember having this feeling of excitement—I felt like I was the first person in my family to ever discover the joys of owning a plant, never really considering that I had grown up in a home filled with plants my parents took care of, that existed there long before my cactus did (and some that existed there long before even I did). I don't know how I never really noticed, never really saw them, until this point. I suppose I never saw my parents as plant-owners, as plant-carer-fors, until it somehow directly affected me.

During my visit, I tell my parents about this exciting new idea I came up with where I one day plan on taking a cutting from their jade plant and growing a new jade plant from it in my own apartment, so that something they took care of every day could beget something that I would take care of every day, which feels like a small and distant way for me to care for them by keeping a piece of their care alive.

My parents smile and tell me that's how they got their plant in the first place, from growing a cutting they had gotten from a dear and old friend.

On staying with friends

Most of my friends live in places far away from where I live, and I feel a specific sense of gratitude about that. And that isn't to say that I feel lucky for not having friends nearby who I have to see all the time—I just mean that when I have to travel, I'm lucky to have friends who I can stay with in some of the places I go. Whenever I am in an unfamiliar city, I prefer staying at a friend's. To do so feels like a special kind of knowing them, and a special kind of feeling at home.

If a home is who you are, in a way, rendered physically and externally, then to stay at a friend's home is to stay not only with them but also among them, surrounded by this external expression of them.

When I stay at a friend's place, the space between saying good night and good morning is an unfamiliar type of quiet. I think it's because it's not my own quiet that I feel in this space, but theirs. On the couch, or the air mattress, or in the guest room, in the dark, it feels like I am borrowing the ordinary quietness they feel every day. I am borrowing their sadnesses, their lonely and still moments, their pauses.

I can feel their *stuff* all around me. Their plants, their books, the furniture they chose, the furniture they didn't have much of a choice in choosing but decided that it was acceptable enough to live with.

This stuff, I believe, is what holds a person. It's where you store yourself, in a way, to define and then to remember who you are.

And in the morning, all this stuff reanimates its owner, reminding them of themself. And when I wake up around my friend's stuff, it feels like now their stuff is animating me as well. Only, I'm a bit different now. I wake up, not with my own stuff reinvigorating and reassembling "Me" but with my friend's stuff, so it feels like I wake up *as* them, a little bit. And then I start the day—it's so rare to start the day not as yourself—as they do. And through this, I feel like I am a little closer to them.

This is nice, except that what follows this closeness of staying with a friend is the inevitable act of leaving them, leaving their home, leaving their city, as one must after they are done visiting. And I will leave them the same way they leave their home every day, this being the last feeling of closeness I feel to them for a little while, because in visiting them, there was a deadline to this specific closeness—there were only a finite number of days I could see them in person—whereas after I leave, we might not speak to each other for months, sometimes even years, knowing that we are always one message away from each other but the ease of *that* closeness means we can talk at any time, and so there is no specific urgency to do so, and so we put it off, and we put it off, and we put it off.

"Friendship"

I am trying to pressure myself less on what a friendship "should" be. Is it not enough to see someone once a year when we live in different cities and one of us is passing through the other's? Or get coffee once a year with a friend who lives in the same city when we are both overwhelmed and underwater with the rest of our lives?

I've never been sure what friendship even is, but even so, sometimes I worry, *shouldn't it be more than this?*

I know that I have friends who I have spent time with in person maybe three times in my life, who I met through social media out of a mutual respect and admiration for each other, who I text a few times every week, who feel incredibly close to me.

Are friends supposed to be people I see in person on a regular basis? Am I supposed to hang out with my friends in a coffee shop in New York for a few hours every day? Am I supposed to even talk to my friends every day? And do text messages count in that? Does saying hi every so often in a group chat count? And if they don't respond, does that still count because I did the reaching out anyway? I don't begrudge anyone for not responding and not getting back to me, because I do that, too. I understand other things get in the way, or that sometimes, the burden of configuring a response that encompasses everything that needs to be said is too great to face at the moment.

Who or what is influencing my thinking on what friendship "should" look like, anyway? Where did I learn that from, and why do I give that authority over my own experiences? Is there some standard for friendship that I internalized from a kids' show, decades ago, before the internet, before I grew up into a world that a kids' show never could have predicted, that I somehow still hold myself to? If my friendships don't adhere to the expectations I've learned from TV, from media, from hearing stories about other peoples' close friendships, then does it mean I don't have any "real" friends? Or do those expectations just make me feel guilty, or make me feel like the relationships I have with the people I care about are not enough, are never enough, will never be enough?

Perhaps the expectation of what friendship "should" be is ruining whatever semblances of friendship I do have. Maybe what I have—maybe a few texts a week, seeing someone once a year— maybe that's it. Maybe that's friendship enough.

I do know that as I and all my friends are squeezed by this pressure to work in all aspects of our lives, everything and everyone else suffers and is squeezed out. I know that includes friendships. And everyone is so busy and under immense pressure trying to survive that I think we are collectively doing our best.

I think I am better off just calling friendship by whatever it is that I have to call it by. If it feels like friendship, and I enjoy it, and I feel fulfilled by it, perhaps that's what it is. Perhaps I am safe to call it that. What else is there to go by, right?

Or am I giving up?

A conversation with a close friend who I haven't spoken to now in years

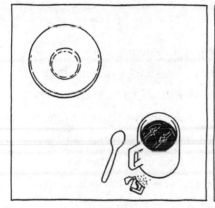

...Maybe that's
happiness.

On nostalgia

I have a certain nostalgia for happy moments, from years and years ago, that I do not remember feeling happy during. Perhaps happiness flees so quickly after it visits that I forget that it even visited at all, and so I am just left remembering happy moments as times when I should have been happy, forgetting that I actually did feel happy, but it came and left so quickly that it was as if it didn't come in the first place. Or, perhaps, what's closer to the truth is that I didn't feel happy in those moments at all.

Instead, what I can only seem to remember is the anxiety and worry I felt during those moments. The happiness comes much later—it is what comes now, years and years after, when I can convince myself that I can finally, safely feel happy about those moments because all those worries and anxieties did not seem to bear any fruit. The good thing that was Really Happening didn't fall to pieces or get taken away from me or get crossed out by something I did or something bad happening the following day, or the following month, or in the following years. The memory is still standing. The good thing still

Really Happened. And enough time has passed to be safe to say, "Yes, you would have been justified in feeling happy at that moment." And that feels pretty close to having a memory of actually feeling happy back then.

It feels pretty close because it is to look back and try to re-assure myself, "Now that it is over and it has happened, it is safe to finally feel the happiness you wanted to feel about it. Now you can feel happy because now your happiness will not get in the way, will not change the outcome, it cannot ruin it somehow in the way you think that happiness might, because it's already happened. It's locked away in the past. The memory has finally hardened into stone."

So this nostalgia is, what, an echo of a happiness? Or a long-delayed one? Is it an outline of one, from trying to remember a happiness I knew I should have felt in the moment but that most likely wasn't really there? Or, maybe nostalgia is to feel a happiness about something that is over *because* it is over. That in order to feel happy about it, it must be something that you can't go back to and affect, that you can't mess up from where you are now, but also, that you can't really feel at all.

You used to be such a happy child

When my mom sometimes sighs and says, "You used to be such a happy child," which part is being mourned as having "used to be"? "You used to be a child," I suppose, is sad in itself, in the way that time passing is often sad. But everyone aside from babies used to be a child, so it can't be that sad. "You used to be happy" is what it feels like that phrase really means. "Why aren't you happy anymore?" is what that phrase feels like it's asking.

I have started to notice that, in describing my brother's childhood, my mom likes to say, "You were always such a happy child."

Eureka

On some rare, special mornings, I wake up with some rare, special idea. It feels like my brain had been working on this idea all night as I was sleeping, trying to meet this deadline of the morning, and it wakes me up, shouting,

HERE IT IS. I DID IT. I CAME UP
WITH SOMETHING GREAT FOR
YOU!

And by the time I get out of bed, that shouting becomes,

WELL, OKAY, I KNOW THERE ARE
A FEW HOLES IN IT BUT THIS IS
THE BEST I COULD DO WITHOUT
YOU CONSCIOUSLY AT THE WHEEL
TELLING ME WHERE TO GO.

And then as the day goes on, that becomes,

OKAY, I'M SORRY IT'S NOT GREAT BUT AT LEAST IT'S SOMETHING, RIGHT?

And by the end of the day, that turns into something like,

OKAY, OKAY. SO I KNOW I DIDN'T HIT THE MARK, LIKE, AT ALL, BUT AT LEAST I TRIED, RIGHT? I MEAN, HEY! EVEN *YOU* THOUGHT THE PHRASE "JURASSIC PARK, BUT WITH DINOSAUR-SIZED FROGS" WAS A GREAT IDEA WHEN YOU WOKE UP!

And I always try to hang on to whatever that idea is for as long as I can, just in *case* it's a good one, but eventually I come to a point where I must face the truth. My brain is the same as I am when I scramble to meet a deadline by delivering some lackluster product that I try to pass off as thought-out and well-considered.

But even if the idea doesn't make sense, I still value it because that *feeling* of having figured something out is one that I find myself enjoying, even when the thing that has been figured out reveals itself to not be anything at all. My dreaming brain hasn't given me an idea to work with, but it's given me a feeling to chase. Getting that feeling when I am awake, through working on something that actually *does* get figured out, makes me happy, which I guess means that working sometimes makes me happy. And it troubles me that this is the thing that makes me feel happier than waking up, happier than falling asleep, happier than dreaming in any form at all.

On peace

Deadlines bring me some form of happiness, too, I suppose, in the form of a kind of peace. Having a deadline looming is almost a peaceful thing because it feels as if the deadline simplifies all the variables of living. It forces everything not deadline-related to blur out of focus.

Without a deadline, time feels too open to be peaceful. That freedom is crushing because it feels like looking at a big, blank canvas of usable time, and then being forced to solve how to use it best. It takes so much work just to get to figuring out what to do with the time! There are too many possibilities, too much potential, and by extension, too much pressure. Because what if I do the wrong thing? What if I squander the options? Is now the time to work? And if so, what do I work on? Is now the time to rest? And if it is, how can I rest in the best way possible? How do I get the *most* rest? But if it is time to rest, doesn't this mean that I can use this time to be not resting instead? And so I feel like I can only find peace within focused and defined time. Without a focus, all that undefined time causes me to freeze as

I try to calculate and plan and decide in my head on what the most worthwhile thing to spend my time on would be, and then suddenly I look up and the day is over and I've squandered my day anyway, lost to the promise of potential.

But on deadline days, and the days leading up to a deadline, it feels like all of that falls away—the deadline shuts everything else out—and I feel magically able to focus on the thing that is the most pressing, and with that comes a solace from the fears that I am not using my time to its greatest potential. The magic that brings this about is just pressure, but a different kind of pressure than the seemingly unsolvable pressure of having undefined time. The peace that comes with having your time be defined by a deadline is that the deadline presents you with only one way to use your time and says there is only one thing you can do in order to relieve this pressure, and so you stop worrying about *how* to use your time, and are finally free to just go about using it.

And I am bothered by the fact that my feeling peace requires an external trigger, and worse, that the external trigger required is work. But for all the stress that deadlines bring, they also promise: "Don't worry about everything else. This is what's important. Trust me." And I enjoy believing it. It is a soothing lie.

Making rest

The only way I feel able to take a break is if I stay up all night working, or if I stay up for multiple nights working, until I finally exhaust myself physically and mentally to the point where I am forced to stop working, because I am incapable of producing any more usable work, at least for a day

I fear that I have learned to look forward to burning myself out like this, to love this numbed exhaustion, because it is the closest thing I can get to some form of rest.

And I'm sad that this is the only way I allow myself to actually take the rest, because it is the only circumstance in which I can see rest as productive, in that resting at this point is the only way I can get myself back into working shape once again.

Building blocks

I feel as though my life should feel like I'm building something, like I'm laying blocks on top of blocks and building a foundation, then a structure upon that, then a roof upon that, so it becomes a house, a school, a library, something that can stand and last. But it feels more to me like playing Tetris.

Tetris has always fascinated me because, look, if you gave anyone an empty grid and a set of blocks of varying shapes with no other context, I would assume that most people would think that the objective of the game was to fill the grid with the blocks fitting perfectly into each other, positioning the shapes to build a solid wall without any gaps in it. This is absolutely what I thought the goal of the game was when I was a kid, the first time I played it at my cousin's house. In Tetris, though—to the surprise of a six-year-old me—as soon as you do a good job, as soon as you complete a row without any gaps, the good job vanishes! Within the grid, you lose proof that you did anything at all, and things just get harder and the blocks come down faster and any good job you do of fitting *those* blocks together perfectly disappears as well! And as a kid, I didn't figure out that there was a little number in the corner of the screen to serve as proof that I was progressing—I was too busy focusing on and panicking about fitting the falling blocks together! And panicking over why they just kept disappearing! I was confused about how the only way to fill the grid up with blocks, to build any sort of lasting structure on the screen, was to do a terrible job!

And now, work feels very much the same. I think I am trying to build myself up with what I work on, but when I finish any task, when I complete a row on the screen, instead of it being a layer to build this lasting foundation upon, it feels like the project just disappears—it's in the past, it's gone, it does not add to who I am, and suddenly I am just faced with another blank row, starting from nothing again.

It feels like any work stops being part of me as soon as it's complete. It's taken from within me to be outside of me, and then it's no longer mine, and it no longer feels like it defines me.

And so in an effort to gain any sort of lasting sense of self, I try now to keep as many incomplete things on my screen as I can so I can show myself: This Is Who You Are Right Now. And it's hard to intentionally keep the screen full of holes instead of completing the rows, but these incomplete rows are the proof that I'm working on something and they are the proof that I exist and they are there to prevent me from ever feeling like I am staring at a blank screen, worrying if I'll ever be able to fill this emptiness again.

But to do so also means accepting a fear that never goes away, the promise that if I keep too many incomplete rows going, things will get out of hand and the blocks will keep falling and the screen will get full and then the game is over.

Is it a living or is it alive?

I am trying to catch myself more whenever I think about work as something that is alive. When work is "pressuring" someone, or "growing," or "needs attention," what does that mean? I am all for giving life to inanimate objects, but to anthropomorphize work feels different, more dangerous to me. I think that maybe I imbue or I have learned to imbue work with this idea of life because I need to work to survive. And if I have to work instead of live, the work itself might as well live, since I apparently cannot.

Part 2: Go Slow

Air plant

Once, after I had moved away from somewhere I had called home, while I was still trying to get settled into an unfamiliar place and feeling like I didn't know how to get myself to feel better, I bought an air plant because I thought that maybe it would bring me happiness, and I assumed that even if it didn't really do that, that at least it would be easy to care for, that I didn't need to do anything for it to stay alive, that, as its name suggests, as long as it has air, it will have everything it needs. After a great deal of research, I learned that air plants need care just like every plant does. They need to be watered, and the commonly accepted practice of misting them is usually not enough. One recommended way to care for an air plant is to give it a deep soak in water every week, for about 15 minutes or 30 minutes or 45 minutes depending on the type of air plant you have and the plant care website and/or book you are getting your information from. I learned that this helps because air plants grow naturally in very humid environments (like a rain forest) and get a lot of water from the air, and so they actually need a lot of water to thrive in less humid environments (like a room).

One risk to this method is that water droplets might get caught in the center of an air plant, among the bases of its densely packed leaves, and this may cause the base of the plant to rot. One way to avoid this is to, after soaking it, let the plant dry upside down, so the water eventually flows down the leaves, away from the center, and evaporates into the air. To help this process, some sources recommend holding it firmly but carefully by the base and giving it a few solid shakes after soaking it to loosen the water droplets away.

I found that giving my air plant a weekly bath was a calming routine for me, and grew used to gently shaking the plant out afterward and setting it upside down to dry. One day, after several months had passed of settling into this routine, I shook it too hard, too used to the routine that I did not give this shaking the appropriate amount of gentle attention it required. I knew I shook it too hard because some of the leaves growing out of the center of the plant flew out, detaching, leaving a hole in its center! I screamed. I was horrified. *I was a monster!*

One thing about air plants is that if you don't water them enough, their tips start to brown and pinch, and they get curlier and curlier. This is a change that happens over much longer periods compared to most other plants, over months instead of days, and it reminds me that even among plants, which already seem to move slowly, some move at a much slower pace than others. I had noticed that my air plant would sometimes get curlier when it hadn't been watered, and I would subtly adjust its watering schedule in response to seeing that some of its tips had started browning, at different times over the many months I cared for it before the day I shook out its center leaves.

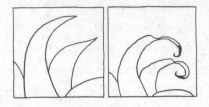

And now, I didn't know if I killed my plant in this one swift action or not. It was still the same pale green color, and in fact looked exactly the same as it did before, only without some of its leaves in its center. I did not want to, or could not bear to, wait for months in order to find out how much damage I had done to it, by watching my plant either die a creeping, impossibly slow death through observing its tips browning and drying out a little bit more and a little bit more and a little bit more, or by seeing it continue to look exactly the same, with me wondering, *Does this mean it's okay? Is it surviving? Or is it dying much more slowly than I thought it would?*

And so I threw it out, choosing the immediate and sharp pang of remorse over the much duller but much deeper one that would have been more drawn out but perhaps less guaranteed.

How to cook scrambled eggs

Eggs
Oil or butter
Pan
Heat
Thoughts

Place a pan on the stove and set the heat to the lowest setting.

Wait for the pan to get a little, tiny bit warm, then add oil or melt butter into the pan.

Meanwhile, crack eggs into a bowl and whisk them until smooth.

Pour the whisked eggs into the very slightly warmed pan, and stir slowly, constantly.

Keep stirring the raw egg fluid.

Keep stirring the raw egg fluid.

Never stop stirring the raw egg fluid.

Stir, noting that if it doesn't look like anything is happening at all, that means you're on the right track.

Stir, noting that if it looks like nothing will ever change, that means you're doing it right.

Keep stirring the raw egg fluid. Stare at the eggs you're stirring until you forget everything else. There is only the egg fluid. Watch it swirl as you stir it. Never stop stirring! As soon as you stop, the eggs will set and burn. Just keep stirring! Keep zoning into the egg cyclone until you forget that you are the one stirring it, and until you forget yourself.

Let the yellow raw egg juice be what centers you. Let your mind swirl the way the raw eggy glob swirls around the pan. You're in egg world now. Everything is eggs.

Stir, thinking of eggs.

Stir, scrambling your thoughts of eggs.

HOW TO COOK A TEA EGG

Eggs
Tea (?)
Brown glass pot
Dad
Coloring book
Toys

Sit at the kitchen island as you read, as you draw, as you play with your toys.

Watch a brown glass pot full of eggs in a dark brown liquid simmer for hours on the stove.

Wonder if the brown liquid is somehow why the entire glass pot is brown.

Wait until a salty, earthy smell fills the kitchen.

Watch as your dad takes an egg out from this pot.

Have a peeled hard-boiled egg, its entire
egg-white surface stained in a cracked brown
web-like pattern, placed in front of you.

Slice in half, revealing a hard-boiled
yellow yolk, a bit gray around its edges where
it meets the egg white.

Eat every morning.

Savor.

HOW TO COOK A RAW EGG OVER RICE

Egg
Rice
Soy sauce
Mom
Brother
Elementary
school video
about foods
of the world

On your way to school, listen to your brother
say that *athletes* eat raw eggs, so why can't we?

Listen to your mom say, from the driver's
seat, that it's not safe to eat raw eggs.

After school, listen to your brother
excitedly recite a recipe he learned for *tamago
kake gohan*, a traditional Japanese dish from a
video he watched in class today:

1. Cook rice.

2. Immediately after, as the rice is still hot,
crack egg onto rice, add soy sauce, and stir
vigorously so the egg coats the rice.

3. Eat while hot.

Watch as your brother cracks a raw egg
into a bowl of room-temperature rice instead
of freshly cooked, hot rice.

Watch as your brother pours soy sauce
over it and stirs vigorously.

Watch as your brother eats, and says it's delicious.

Watch as your brother throws up.

Listen to your mom say, "This is why we don't eat raw eggs!"

HOW TO COOK A STEAMED EGG

Egg
Water
Soy sauce
Sesame oil
Small bowl
Large pot
Spoon
Mom

Throw up, but because you have the flu, not because you ate a raw egg.

Stay in bed and miss school.

Watch as your mom cracks an egg into a small bowl and whisks it, then watch as she gently adds water in with the beaten egg and whisks it again, to combine.

Watch as your mom brings a large pot with a shallow layer of water to a simmer, then places the bowl with the whisked egg into the pot and covers it, so the steam from the simmering water cooks the egg mixture in the bowl.

Watch as your mom takes the bowl out and puts it in front of you, and observe the smooth, flat surface of the egg in the bowl, now set into a jiggly, soft, custardy texture.

Top with soy sauce and sesame oil.

Eat, noticing how smooth and silky the egg is, as if it isn't even an egg at all.

Feel better, a little bit.

HOW TO COOK A HARD-BOILED EGG

Egg
Soy sauce
(optional)
Chili garlic
sauce
(optional)
Salt (optional)
Pepper
(optional)
Plate
Dad
Computer lab
Webcomic

Wake up late for class to your dad shouting at you from the kitchen to get up.

Sit down to a plate of hard-boiled eggs he made for you, sliced into quarters.

Top with soy sauce and the chili garlic sauce with the rooster logo on the plastic jar with the green lid and eat.

Alternatively, top with salt and pepper and eat.

Surfing the internet at the computer lab between classes, come across a webcomic that describes all the ways to cook an egg. Do not know what soft-boiled means. Or sunny-side up. Or poached.

When you see hard-boiled described in this comic, notice that the caption reads: (aka "ruin it").

Wonder what's wrong with hard-boiled eggs.

HOW TO COOK A 1,000-YEAR-OLD EGG

1,000-year-old
egg
Congee
(optional)
Soy sauce
Sesame oil
Mom

Order congee from one of your mom's favorite restaurants and eat all the chunks of 1,000-year-old egg cooked into it.

Alternatively, go find a pack of four 1,000-year-old eggs, packed in a Styrofoam case, when you go with your parents to the store in Chinatown that they get groceries from. Bring it to your mom and sometimes, she will buy it, as a treat.

Sit down to a plate of 1,000-year-old eggs, sliced into chunks, topped with soy sauce and sesame oil. Eat. Savor.

Ask if they are really one thousand years old. Believe whatever answer your mom gives you.

HOW TO COOK A SOFT-BOILED EGG

Egg
Friends
Restaurants
Internet
Water
Steam
Microwave
timer
Spoon
Loved one

Get older.

Go out with your friends to brunch restaurants. Meet your friends for breakfast. Enjoy eggs Benedict. Be suspicious of the runny yolk at first, but over time, learn that it is safe to eat, and enjoy it. Order eggs "over easy." Order eggs "sunny-side up." Learn in private what all these things mean so you know what you are ordering next time you go.

Love the runny yolk.

Move out. Live on your own.

Buy eggs because they are cheap and a good source of protein and have a long fridge life.

Learn all the different methods of boiling a perfect soft-boiled egg. Every morning, choose a different method. Research methods

for too long every morning, and let hours pass,
and then look up at the time and realize it is
one in the afternoon and be incredibly hungry.

Don't place a cold egg into boiling water,
it might crack.

Don't place an egg in water and bring
it to a boil then turn it off. Boiled water
cools inconsistently and the result won't be
consistent each time.

Bring half an inch of water in a small pot
to a boil. Lower the heat to a simmer.

Place egg in pot, straight from the fridge,
and cover with lid.

Let the simmering water fill the pot
with steam, so you are steaming the egg
instead of boiling it. Steam stays a consistent
temperature, unlike water, and so steaming
will be consistent.

Steam egg for exactly 6 minutes and 40
seconds.

Run egg under cold water until cooled
down.

Crack egg with spoon all the way around,
then peel.

Eat over the sink, pouring a bit of soy
sauce on each bite. Eat, placing egg in a
bowl of instant ramen. Eat with quinoa and
greens.

Later, live with your loved one.

Make soft-boiled eggs in the morning,

trying to impress your loved one by carefully
cracking each egg all the way around by
tapping the entire surface of the shell with
the back of a spoon, so that when you peel the
egg, the shell comes off the egg easily without
any pieces of eggshell stuck to the cooked egg.

Listen to your loved one ask you why you
peel eggs that way.

Ask, "Doesn't everyone? It makes so much
sense."

Listen to your loved one say, "No, I've
never seen it done that way."

Realize you do not know.

Wonder why you crack eggs this way.

HOW TO COOK A TEA EGG

Egg
Tea (?)

Remember, for a brief second, how you used to
eat tea eggs as a child.

Forget.

Go about your day.

HOW TO COOK A SCRAMBLED EGG IN FRIED RICE

Egg
Oil
Rice
Pan
Phone
Parents

Answer the FaceTime from your mom and tell
her that you're making eggs for dinner.

Listen as your mom asks if you are eating
enough, if you are eating meat with that,
if you are eating enough veggies, if you are
eating enough carbs, too. Listen to her suggest

fried rice as something you can make tonight, because there are eggs in that. "You can make it mama's way. Dad will explain."

Watch as she shoves her phone in front of your dad and listen as he tells you how to scramble eggs in fried rice even though you don't really make fried rice that much and you are busy and you don't have time to listen to him tell you this.

"The secret is in the eggs," he says. "The secret is to cook the egg directly in the pan after the rice is fried."

Hear your mom from outside of the frame: "Make sure the pan is on high heat."

Make fried rice, making sure the pan is on high heat.

After the rice is done, push it to the sides of the pan to expose the surface of the pan in the middle.

Pour oil where the pan is exposed.

Crack eggs into a separate bowl and beat eggs, then pour them onto the hot oil on the exposed part of the pan on high heat.

Move quickly as the eggs set immediately, folding eggs into loose sheets and clumps, then combine with the fried rice until evenly distributed.

This will lead to perfect, fully-cooked-through scrambled eggs that are not raw at all.

HOW TO COOK A TEA EGG

Tea egg vendor
Tea egg
Tea (?)
Loved one
Engagement ring
Wedding ring
Dim sum restaurant
Parents
Family group chat
A feeling of closeness

Walk with your loved one through Chinatown and smell something familiar.

Approach the stall with a vendor selling tea eggs on the street.

Remember how much you ate tea eggs growing up.

Buy a few and share them, eager and trusting that she will like them.

Watch her savor a new food for the first time.

Later, get engaged.

Later, at lunch one day before the wedding, ask your parents how to make tea eggs.

Be surprised by how excited your dad is and how proud your mom is to tell you.

Be so surprised by this rare display of excitement and pride that you later realize you did not take in anything they said, but don't let this bother you because of how nice you felt in hearing them tell you about it together.

Later, a few months after the wedding, in the family group chat, text your parents and ask how to make them.

Read your dad's message, because he usually responds quicker: "Okay. It is your mom's recipe, but I will type up the instructions. Follow them carefully. But most importantly, remember that they have to sit for a few days before you eat them."

Read your mom's text interjection: "I always eat them right away before they get a chance to absorb all the salt and flavor."

Watch as your brother reacts to this message with the "ha! ha!" reaction.

Read your dad's response: "That is why I always had to cook so many, because you would eat them before they were ready."

Watch as your brother reacts to *this* message with the "ha! ha!" reaction.

Smile, as you realize how watching this bickering text exchange makes you feel like you are in the same room as them.

Watch your screen as your dad texts message after message after message, a far-too-detailed set of instructions for what should be a simple recipe, and understand that he is doing this partly because your mom is sitting next to him telling him what to write and he is trying to get it all down properly, and partly because he doesn't want you to be disappointed in case you misinterpret something he says and you get something wrong.

Realize how, after all these years, you thought that making tea eggs was something you were just supposed to figure out yourself, or something that you were just supposed to have absorbed from your parents in some unspoken passing of intergenerational knowledge. But all you really needed to do was ask.

HOW TO COOK A TEA EGG

Eggs
Cold water
Large pot
Spoon
The plastic shopping bag full of packets of black tea given to you by your father the last time you visited home
Salt
Star anise (optional)
Chinese prickly ash (optional)
27 text messages, assorted lengths

Okay, son. It's quite easy.

Rinse a dozen or two dozen eggs in cold water first, so the shells aren't dirty. If they are dirty, the water will get dirty, which will make the eggs dirty.

Put the eggs in a large pot of cold water, then bring them to boiling, high heat is fine, but doesn't need to be max. Once it boils for a few minutes (3 to 5 minutes is fine), turn off the heat and take it off the heat.

Take the eggs out of the hot water with a spoon or so (do not pour the hot water out of the pot because you use that hot water to make the tea), and put the eggs in a bowl under running cold water in the sink to cool them down, but don't run the water too strongly because you don't want to waste water. Do this for a few minutes (3 to 5 minutes is fine) until the eggs are cool enough to touch and hold in your hands.

Meanwhile, add tea leaves, salt, star anise, Chinese prickly ash (Sichuan peppercorn, but your mom calls it Chinese prickly ash, so that's what I will call it for this recipe) to the pot of boiled water. If you do not have the spices, that is okay. You can still make it. The most important parts are tea leaves and salt. Use the tea packets I gave you. You should still have them. I gave you a big bag of them; did you take them with you when you left? The tea is what gives it the flavor. That is the way we used to always make it for you.

You make the tea in the pot because you are going to put the eggs back in the pot and then simmer the eggs in the salty tea in the pot for hours, so they soak up all the flavor and get salted and delicious. After a few hours (3 to 5 hours is fine), put the pot, with the eggs in the tea, in the fridge overnight, and for as long as they remain uneaten. They will get tastier every day, so the trick is to try not to eat them all in the first two days like your mom does. Let them soak for a few days (3 to 5 days is fine).

But before all that, in order for the eggs to absorb the flavor, you can't leave the eggs like they are when you take them out of the pot. You need to crack the shells all around the egg so when you simmer them in the tea, the tea can get into the egg through the cracks.

So after you boil the eggs, when the eggs are cool enough to touch and hold in your hands, take a spoon and gently tap the eggshell all the way around, cracking the shell

uniformly over the whole egg, but not having
it come off the egg, and not removing the
eggshell.

HOW TO CRACK A BOILED EGG

Self

Look up from reading your dad's texts.

Suddenly realize that this is why you
crack your eggs this way.

Try to hold back whatever this feeling is.

HOW TO FINISH COOKING SCRAMBLED EGGS

Eggs
Oil or butter
Pan
Heat
Thoughts

Without warning, the raw egg fluid you are
stirring will suddenly start to become translucent, gooey curds. Keep stirring! Don't let
them set. When they are still gooey but no
longer translucent, they are done. Congratula-
tions! Don't let them set and become too dry.

Take your perfectly gooey scrambled eggs
off the heat and serve immediately. Make a
note of how much time has passed since you
started, maybe 6 or 7 minutes, and realize that
it felt like you were gone for hours.

Serve on rice with Lao Gan Ma, serve on
toast with some avocado and hot sauce, serve
in a tortilla with jalapeño and sour cream,
serve plain.

Eat, imagining that the sheer energy of

your thoughts is what convinced the eggs to
eventually become scrambled.

Eat, thinking about how all things
undergo change, that this is the nature of
everything.

Eat, imagining that the eggs absorbed
all the memories you called up while making
them, and by eating them, you are welcoming
everything you remembered back into you.

A place to visit without being a visitor

Leaving a restaurant that my parents had chosen to go to delights me because they always somehow know the owners and all the waitstaff, even in the cases when they told me this restaurant opened just a few weeks ago.

It's in the leaving that this fact reveals itself, when everyone from the kitchen and the back room comes out to make conversation, to ask if everything was delicious, to say goodbye, to—if this is a restaurant we've come to for years—say how much my brother and I have grown, or to—if this is a restaurant that just opened a few weeks ago—say how lovely it is that my brother and I were finally able to come and visit and eat, that they had all heard so much about us from our parents. All in all, a joyous, boisterous exit.

My parents have a way of knowing every time a new Chinese restaurant opens in Toronto, and will—it seems to me— have tried them all by the time they open, and will have decided on a detailed review of each of them ("very good" or "too oily" or "too salty" or "better, but a higher price" or "worse *and* a higher price"), and then will exclusively go to the ones that they deem their favorites, until they are friends with the owners, chefs, and entire waitstaffs. (It seems to be that their favorite restaurants are often the ones where all three roles are held by the same person.)

Every time I visit, there will be a new dumpling house, or a new dim sum place, or a new noodle place that they *have* to take me to, because they became friends with the owner (who is also often the chef and who is also often the front of house). And I'd get annoyed with how, if the restaurant was open and running but that person wasn't around—if only their husband was, or if only one of their kids was, or if only their staff was—my parents would turn around and leave and come back later when that person was there.

I used to think it was because they wanted to show me off— "Look at our kids!" or "Look at my son!" But I think there is a part of them that is also showing themselves off to me—"Look, your parents are people of the town. We are people who people know! And people like us!"

I am certain, too, that there is an element of "this is someone who I can talk to, to support, to bring my business to." My parents often like to go to Chinese restaurants, and I used to think this was related to a dietary pickiness, but I am learning that they just want to go places where they know they will be interacting with and supporting people who will talk to them like people, who will treat them and see them as whole. To be Asian in (North) America is to keep a short running list of places where you know you will be given the gift of being seen as more than a visitor.

When I see my parents laughing and catching up with the people who run these restaurants, I think about their insistence that they are *friends* with them. I have always imagined that being regulars at a restaurant would be described more as patronage, but it feels like my parents occupy something that is more than that, and I find myself wondering what the bounds are that would slip that relationship into what could safely be called a friendship. A now-distant friend of mine from high school had a long-standing fantasy to be able to go to their local burger place and say *I'll Have The Usual* and have everyone working there recognize them and greet them and know them by name and know their order and know what *The Usual* meant (in their case, a hamburger with the specific toppings they liked). In retrospect, perhaps this was one of those desires that we have when we are younger that we don't really understand the meaning of until we grow up. At that age, perhaps, we'd already absorbed and found a way to articulate one of the more enticing promises of capitalism—of buying, or spending, your way into belonging. And this friend was very excited about the ability to do so, which meant that they were very cynical or very shrewd or very naive. And I understand now that this came from being young and wanting to be seen, remembered, perhaps to feel some tiny grasp of a little bit of control, but mainly to have one more place on the (very) short list of places where you feel you might belong.

And is it friendship or patronage that describes what it is between someone you make an effort to see whenever you can, who makes you feel welcome and seen, who you feign joyousness with even on joyless days, who you catch up with and want to support as best as possible? "You're not friends, you're customers," I said once to my mom. "We can be customers anywhere," she says back after a long moment of thought, "but we choose to go back to the same places for a reason."

My brother lives in Cambridge now, which is where I once lived, too, in my basement—sorry, *Garden-Level*—apartment, though I had moved away before he moved there. The last time

I visited him in Cambridge, we lined up for thirty minutes at a restaurant I missed dearly—a little udon spot in the back of a college food court, which made the most perfect bowl of spicy cold niku udon I've ever had. I was excited. We reach the middle of the line when Sara, the marketing manager who also runs the front of house recognizes me. We talk and catch up. They run the restaurant's account on Instagram and we follow each other so they know what I'm up to, I tell my brother after clocking his surprise as Sara asks me very specific things about my life. "How is LA? What are you cooking? How are your plants?"

The udon place is an open-concept stand where you can see the cooking happening from the seats and Sara seats us in the back row. I crane my head to see if the head chef, Tomo, is back there. I want to wave to him and tell him that I love his udon, and because last time I was here I came by myself for a quick bowl in between meetings and we talked as I ate and he gave me extra hot chili oil for my udon and told me how they make it in-house and how I can always ask for more and I do. "Is Tomo around?" "Oh, he just stepped out."

We finish our meal and Tomo still hasn't come back and I leave feeling a little disappointed.

As we step out of the food court building, I send Tomo a message on Instagram because we follow each other, too: "I came by with my brother! I just missed you!" and he messages back, and I stop and smile and say, "A ha!" and my brother sighs in a way that I recognize as the exact same sigh I make whenever my parents make sure they talk to the owner and the chef before they leave a restaurant, as I show him my exchange with Tomo on my phone, as if to say to him, "See, I'm a person who people know, and people like me."

Sanctuary

It seems that every dim sum place I have ever gone to consists of ducking under a small doorway, or winding up (or down!) an unassuming service staircase, or getting into a tiny elevator, only to emerge into a gigantic, cavernous, cacophonous space, which seems way too large to fit into the plain-looking regular-size building hiding it, and which seems to willingly defy the most ordinary way you arrived into it. As if to say, *A ha! You weren't expecting* this, *now, were you?*

I never remember these dim sum places as having any windows, though they must, and I think my memory is just being influenced by how it feels like there is no way to understand the passage of time once you are inside, as the food keeps refilling and the dirty plates keep being replaced with clean ones and the empty steamers and dishes in the center of your table get replaced with full ones, and the ladies with the carts seem to always be giving out food but never running out of it, as all the proof of having eaten is constantly swept away to make room for what's next. It always feels like the meal is just beginning.

This is a place where time is of no importance. The fact that you are here, now, is the only important thing. I always feel like I can eat more here, and perhaps that is part of the point, that it was meant to be this way so you can order more, buy more, spend more. But it also feels like a place to escape the rest of the world—here you are outside of time, and outside of the world. This is Dim Sum King, this is New Ho King, this is Ho Won Restaurant, this is Silver Dragon, this is the Only Place That Exists and has ever existed. The only thing that matters is that you are here now, and this is what's in front of you.

And what's in front of you is everything. It is a marketplace where you purchase all these different dishes from so many different vendors, while simultaneously watching these vendors go by between the tables like cars passing you on the street. The space is big and bustling enough to feel like you are outside, that you are in the city, on a sidewalk, in a park, people-watching, while simultaneously being part of the crowd while simultaneously watching over the kids or visiting the old folks or catching up with friends or talking to your brother, while simultaneously visiting an aquarium and watching fish in a tank while simultaneously being under the ocean, while simultaneously *just watching*, being an audience member while at the same time performing, always performing for everyone, to show that you are part of a nice family and that you are a good child who sits up straight and eats politely and doesn't talk with your mouth full of food, while simultaneously being in a waiting room under these fluorescent lights, permanently waiting and being and watching and performing all at the same time. It is a bustling market, a dining room, a family reunion, a kitchen, an extension of your own home, a community center, a day care, a classroom, a theater, all superimposed onto each other, all occupying the same space at once.

Why be anywhere else? Why would you ever leave? The room seems to plead with you. *Everything is right here, please. I brought everything you could ever want directly to you.*

And although I go for dim sum with my family at all times of the year, I seem to only have memories of eating here in the winter, when you escape from the outside world while it is still light out, to enter into this cave where time is suspended and constantly looping. And when you emerge back into the real world, it is evening, but it is only 4 P.M., but it is dark now because that is what afternoons are like in the winter in Toronto, and time doesn't make any sense at all but this time it is comforting because who knows how long you were in there for. This means you successfully escaped from the ordinary, constant, churning movement of the world, and the return to it is always disorienting, in the same way you come out of a movie theater and are surprised that it is still daytime, or surprised that it is midnight, because while you were in there, days passed, years passed, a whole lifetime passed in front of your eyes.

"Go slow"

All my parents' favorite restaurants seem to operate the same way, in that they all have waiting built into them. We have to wait for long periods of time, for us to be seated, for the menu to come by, for us to order, for the food to come, for the dishes to be taken away, for the bill to come, for the bill to come back. These moments say, *You're not leaving for a while. Sit for a moment. Get used to it.*

This is not out of neglect or poor service, but out of some form of love, I believe. It comes from a mutual understanding and agreement between everyone involved that this waiting is, deep down, something we came for, perhaps just as much, if not more than, the food itself. The purpose of all this waiting, it feels like, is to draw our attention and focus inward to what's here with us at this moment—to the meal, to each other. A good restaurant, it feels, is a place to go to enjoy waiting. It is a place where waiting is the point. And my parents enjoy sitting for hours, and it seems they only go to the restaurants that also enjoy this, and believe in this, and who let us wait.

My parents linger at restaurants that seem built for lingering. They always order too much, and after we are full, we let what's left of our meal sit in front of us for hours, it feels, and we will pick at it, but mainly just look at it as we talk and as we sit together—a reminder of what we have eaten already, a symbol that we will never be wanting of anything because look, here it is, here is more if you are still hungry, eat, more, eat. So much of the time I spend with them is walking to a restaurant, then sitting at the table after we are full, lingering, sitting, eating a little more, and then, finally, after *mom, let's go* is muttered more than a handful of times, and after she decides that yes, now is the time to go, and now finally, after we ask for the Styrofoam containers and after we wait for them to arrive at the table and after we scoop all the remaining food into them and stack them and bag them and tie them up to take home in order to extend the meal a few more days, we leave.

When we exit the restaurant, everyone gathers by the door and comes from the back room to tell my parents "man zou, man zou!" which I interpret as *go slow*, but which more accurately translates to something like *walk slowly*, which really means *don't hurt yourself*, which really means *take care*. But I like this blessing of going forth from this place, and back into the real world, into the reality of a life of constantly moving with work and pressure and expectations, with the wish to literally go slowly. As if to say, *See? The rest of your life can be measured and paced out, too—in here, you can sit and wait and then you can eat, and then you can sit and wait some more, and then out there, you can continue on with your life just like you did here.* As if to say, *There can be waiting and slowness built into the rest of it all, too.* As if to say, *It doesn't all need to be so rushed.*

When I take my parents to the places I like, they always feel rushed. They say things like, "They brought the bill as soon as we set our utensils down!" and "We just finished eating! Where is the time to sit? To order more?" and "There wasn't enough food! We ate it all! Where are the leftovers?" and "How can we sit and wait and digest, then eat a second round here if we ate all our food in the first round?" and "Aren't you still hungry?"

And I used to be annoyed by their insistence to sit too long, to eat too fully, but now I realize, maybe this becomes the point: The leaving is more joyous when you have become too full of the place where you are. Or maybe that is only my takeaway, and it is completely different from the way they feel, which is: *I wish I could sit here with my son forever, I wish I could hold him with this food and convince him he is still hungry for a few bites more, for a few minutes longer, please stay, please be hungry, please eat, please eat, please eat.*

Layover

I'm currently writing in an airport. Not because I'm waiting for a flight, not because I'm waiting for someone to land, but because I just got off a plane and I am in this new city I've moved to and I have nowhere else really to be. I don't know many people here and I've been subletting someone's room for the last three months and that means that I'm living in someone else's space, so it doesn't comfort me really to start to head over there because I don't see it as a home. So I am forcing a layover, with no flight to catch next, so I can stay here as long as I want.

There is a sense of comfort here, in the airport, precisely because you're not supposed to stay at an airport—the airport is not a destination—you're supposed to spend as little time in an airport as possible. I am very familiar with this feeling that I am not really welcome in a place, and this is a coldness that airports are at least open about. Airports make everyone feel like a passer-through, like a visitor, like an outsider, and this is comforting in its honesty because aren't we always, always just visitors, just passers-through? Most other places try to convince you that you are more than that. Airports don't dress it up.

Because airports make you feel like you're always passing through, it also allows you to feel cut off from the world. While I'm here, I feel actively unreachable, protected by the fact that I am still in transit, still arriving, instead of simply being in this city and having no one in this city who would want to reach me. Here, I don't have to worry about feeling alone for a few moments longer. Feeling lonely is for people who have arrived somewhere, I tell myself, not for people still on the way there.

Escape

I had a dream where I was staring at one of the walls of the room I was subletting when I noticed a crack in the wall, right between where the bed is and where the desk is, and I went up to the crack, and I picked at it, and I picked at it, and it slowly opened up into a hole.

I found myself walking through the hole, only to discover that I did not end up standing in the apartment next door, but that I was inside an impossibly long, expansive hallway with no doors or windows along its sides, and with no way to enter or exit it except for this crack in the wall that I had opened up. It felt like I had accidentally discovered this space backstage to the real world that was never meant to be seen.

I walked down this hallway for what felt like hours, trying to get to the end of it until I realized it had no end, at which point I turned around and climbed back out of the hole and when I was back and safe in the room I was subletting, I discovered that no time had passed at all.

I tried not to enter this hallway—this magic, impossible hallway where time didn't pass—for any reason. It felt wrong.

But in times of stress, it began to feel like the only solution to my problems.

I'd go into it and use it to get some work done, when I was facing an unmeetable deadline, and when I needed more time than I felt I had.

When I went back from it into the world again, it was still the same time as it was when I entered it, only now all my work was finished and I had so much time left in the day to do whatever I wanted. I finally had free time.

But now that I had this hallway available to me, I realized I could use it to get more and more work done.

And so I brought more work in, having all the time I could ever need to do it.

And every time I came back out into the world having completed all my work, I found less and less joy in having all this time outside the hallway to spend my life on.

So instead of taking my newly freed time to live, to connect with people I wanted to know better, to see the world with less guilt, I just used my time outside to hunt for and gather more work, to accumulate it, knowing that I could bring it into my hallway and get it all done and do more. And that became the only thing that felt like it was worth doing in the outside world.

Soon, this hallway held more and more of me. I filled it with things and furniture that helped me get my work done more comfortably.

And one day I brought in enough work to fill an entire life with.

And one day I just didn't come back out.

And the part of this that made it a dream was that no one noticed, because in the outside world, no time was passing at all.

Farm game

My two favorite video games right now are one where I run around doing errands on a farm and another where I run around doing errands on an island. As I play them, I find it relaxing to go on the internet and research what the best crops are, how to get the best items, how and when and where to catch all the fish and bugs, and what schedules the games run on internally so I know how to play them in a way where I can do the most stuff, therefore optimizing my time and achieving the *most productive* relaxation I can. In the island game, special gifts come every five minutes of real-world time, clocking in at :04, then :09, then :14, then :19, and so on, floating in on balloons you have to shoot down from the sky, so every five minutes, I stop whatever it is I'm doing for a moment to run to where they spawn in the hopes I will find one, then I'll go back to what I was doing before, only to check again five minutes later, then five minutes after that, and so on. In the farm game, different crops take a different number of in-game days to grow, which you can then harvest and sell, but after you harvest them you can also pickle them in special pickling jars that I have learned how to make in the game, with each crop taking a different number of in-game days to pickle, at which point I can sell the pickled versions for more money.

Both these games, to Elissa, have no point. "So, what are you supposed to . . . do?" And I try to explain: Everything! There are so many different things to do: crops to grow, wood to chop, rocks to mine, fruit to harvest, fish to catch, bugs to catch, all so you can buy more clothes, so you can build new furniture, so you can make your house bigger.

"Yeah . . . but . . . why?"

There is no real set final goal to either game. They both kind of just . . . keep going. The more time you spend playing, the more money you make, the bigger your house gets, the more stuff you accumulate. It is a lovely fantasy of capitalism, but the enjoyment—the relaxing, calming nature of it—is simply in knowing what to do, and then achieving a desired, reliable outcome in doing it. There is a comfort in knowing these tasks were designed so I could do them, and then, well, doing them. For each game, I have a five-thousand-word list in my phone's notes app that documents all the things I should do in the game every day. And as I play, I like to hold this mental to-do list in my head. Hit these six rocks every day to gain iron, but every five minutes, check for balloons, check for fish in the water and if they are of a certain size then try to catch them, make sure to buy the shop's daily rotating stock before it closes. There is a guarantee designed into these games that promises: if you spend enough time working on this, every task can be achieved. I suppose this is a lovely fantasy of capitalism as well.

When I started taking care of plants in real life, accumulating them in my small apartment in exchange for the money I spent my time making, I made a giant spreadsheet of notes involving their care, making columns for each plant's sunlight needs, moisture levels, soil types, seasonal changes, humidity, ideal temperatures, propagation methods, and schedules of all their watering times. And even with all of this information organized in such a clear, detailed way, some of my plants still died, but if they did, I could convince myself that it wasn't my fault, because I made a *spreadsheet! I put in the work!* I planned it all out perfectly, with my research from the *internet*, so if the plants died, that was on *them*, not me. I *did* my job. And I think what is more relaxing to me than just having all these plants around me is following these watering schedules I had made, researching and then enacting everything in my spreadsheet, which is to say that my favorite ways to relax are to work, just on something other than my work.

Many of my friends have fantasies of quitting their jobs and owning an actual, real-life, physical farm—which is to say that most of my friends are city people, who don't know anything about actual farms. If the fantasy isn't a farm, it's a flower shop, or a garden, or a greenhouse, or, in one case, an arboretum (a fancy name for "tree museum"). So many of my friends are fixated on something to do with nature, involving something that grows, or more accurately, something that *they* can grow, based on the belief that it will be relaxing, and straightforward, and linear, and predictable. I find it curious that these dreams aren't about simply living in and among nature, but they are dreams in which nature is the project we work on. We cannot seem to escape the desire to feel productive with our time. I'm not sure if that's by choice or by trauma, that this pressure to produce has been so engrained in us that our deepest fantasies are still tied to some idea of working on something.

I play my farm game not necessarily because I want to own a real-life, physical farm. It's just that my farm game promises that the work I put into it will have a consistent, measurable result that serves as proof that I put work into it. And maybe that's the same thing that's at the core of my friends' fantasies of some project of nature that they can work on as well. Perhaps after a life of working to no end with no promised outcomes, what we think we want more than anything is to escape into this fantasy that something reliable will happen when we put our time into it. Plant a crop, tend to it, and something will grow.

Part 3: Take Care

The party

I have a fear of going to parties.

The fear isn't that I'll go to the party and know nobody. It's that I'll open the door and see every single person I have ever known at the party without me, all of them not having told me they'd be there. My closest friends, the people I work with, my neighbors, the bus driver, the guy I see on the bus sometimes, the people whose work and careers I admire, my parents, the lady who works at the corner store, the distant friends I went to school with and fell out of touch with, the people I used to pass in the halls, all of them talking to each other and laughing, and laughing, and laughing, confirming this suspicion that I've held all my life that I have been missing out on some secret club that everyone else was a part of. I stand in the doorway and watch them all having fun without me, all of them seeing me standing there but preferring to continue talking to each other, all of them knowing each other better than I have ever known any of them.

Staying in

Here's my idea of a nice social interaction: One afternoon, I become interested in drawing pillows, the way they fold, hold shape, flop over, suggest mass and plumpness and lightness all at once, all through how light and shadow play across their surfaces, and I start painting studies of them, all the different pillows I have in my apartment, and I spend the entire day painting them, folding them and rearranging them, and painting them again, until it is late into the night. It feels rare for me to have the focus for something and the time to focus on it and then to actually focus on it, so I take advantage of it when it happens to me. And today—well—tonight, at 3 A.M. now, that focus is on drawing pillows.

And I feel dumb and a bit strange for caring this much about pillows, and I don't know how I would be able to explain to anyone that I lost a whole day to painting pillows and that I allowed *this* to be the thing that feels urgent to me, and I suddenly feel so utterly alone because who can you talk to about how amazing pillows are when you are suddenly overwhelmed with the desire to paint them? Who else would care about that?

But then, after I'm happy with my studies, I google "pillow studies OR drawings OR paintings" and see that in 1493, the German Renaissance painter Albrecht Dürer had sketched six studies of a pillow on the back of a self-portrait study he had done in preparation for a self-portrait he was painting, the painted self-portrait later being considered by historians to be one of the earliest independent self-portraits in the history of Western painting. The sketches of the pillows on the back of the self-portrait study are concerned with shape, and light, and the folds of the fabric.

And suddenly, I don't feel so strange and alone. There is a comfort in this, in realizing that someone else at some point in time had really cared about the same thing that you do right now, even if that someone was a German Renaissance painter who died five hundred years ago, and the thing you both cared about was how interesting it is that pillows suggest a mass without suggesting a weight, and how you needed to draw them to figure out how they do that. Suddenly, I feel like I am in conversation with someone else, over this very specific topic of interest, only this conversation doesn't happen with a rapid and ongoing exchange of words. It happens with one statement, and then half a millennia later, another one.

Who gets to speak?

Being spoken over and interrupted in most conversations I have been in for most of my life has, I like to think, made me considerate of how much time each person takes (or takes up) in a conversation.

I prefer to talk very little. When it's with someone I care about, I love listening, and I always feel that listening is a better way than talking for me to express my love.

When it's a group conversation, though, I speak very little mainly just from being spoken over all the time. When I realize that the person talking doesn't care about hearing from anyone else, I like to tune out and play the game of counting how long each person in the conversation has talked for. Or of counting how long the speaker has made eye contact with each person in the group. It's a great way to show who the speaker deems important and unimportant in the exchange.

When I recognize someone is being talked over or ignored, or hasn't spoken in a while, I'll try to direct a question or align the conversation toward them. But usually, I'm also a person being talked over or ignored so this doesn't work all too well.

In a recent conversation, catching up with old friends who I adore, I found myself being the one talking the most, and I was incredibly self-conscious of it. I tried to direct the conversation so that other people had the chance to speak, but they'd just direct it back to me, and I felt, after the conversation ended, that I had spoken way too much. I told this to Elissa after, and she said, "I thought you were talking a normal amount," and I realized that I'd been so used to being spoken over, to being cut off, to being conveniently not heard, to not being a major part of most conversations, that maybe a normal amount of talking in a safe and equal conversation made me seem like I was talking way too much.

"But I *was* talking a lot," I said.

"But were you asking questions and wanting to hear about how everyone was doing?" Elissa asked.

"Well, yeah."

"And were they asking about you or were you cutting people off so you could talk?"

"They wanted to hear from me, I guess."

"I think everyone talked the right amount," Elissa said.

"I think Zach didn't talk a lot," I said.

"Well, maybe Zach didn't want to talk that much this time."

And I thought maybe that was right. One thing that makes me really adore someone is seeing that they also use listening as a way to convey love. It is one of the reasons I am friends with Zach, because this is a belief that we both share about conveying attention and presence, and maybe Zach was doing just that. Or maybe there will always be someone spoken over in a conversation. Maybe it will always be unbalanced. Maybe this was a sign that I was not listening enough. I couldn't tell. And it bothered me a lot.

And I realized that this is another reason why I talk very little in most conversations I'm in. The talking is what makes the conversation difficult.

Roulette

Perhaps one benefit ("benefit"?) of my anxiety is that at least I am unsurprised when things don't turn out for the best. I don't necessarily mean this in a "I am always thinking the worst will happen" kind of way (though that is true as well) but more that sudden dramatic downward change is not uncommon, emotionally, in any sense, so I kind of just grew accustomed to sudden dramatic downward changes happening.

Within this anxiety, every moment feels like spinning a roulette wheel. Am I: stressed, terrified, exhausted, EXCITED!, worried, worrying, INSPIRED!, stressed, upset, sad, overcome with guilt over letting people down, overcome with guilt for not working enough, EXCITED AGAIN!, worrying, exhausted, exhausted, exhausted?

Things change so quickly, so it doesn't seem strange to me that something I was really excited about a second ago now fills me with dread, or, maybe worse, apathy. In the exhaustion of this, I have conceded that all this is outside of my control, so in order to cope, I have trained myself to act quickly when the ball in the roulette wheel lands in a "productive" pocket. In that moment, I can capture that feeling and leave the house, or write down the idea, or edit the project, or do the dishes, or do the laundry, or make a meal, or go to bed, and hopefully I can ride that feeling out for at least a little bit before it flips back to terror or numbness. This is the closest thing I have, I think, to some bargained form of discipline. That I am not in control, but at least I can recognize when luck is on my side.

I am trying to decide if I should buy two rolls of paper towel or three

and if I buy two rolls of paper towel now

then they take up less space in the bag that I have to carry home
but

if I buy three rolls of paper towel then I won't have to go buy more rolls of paper towel again as soon as I would if I only bought two and of course there is no right answer
but maybe

if I find myself going back to the store to get more paper towel
sooner I will suddenly be hit with inspiration on the walk there
or hit

by a car on the walk there and

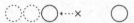

if I got three rolls of paper towel then I would be avoiding that
all together and I
would be more prepared for spills because
what if I only got two rolls of paper towel and ran out and didn't
have enough time to get a new roll of paper towel and then if I
spilled something I'd have to use a sheet of loose-leaf paper to try
to clean it up but that isn't as absorbent and the spill would stain
but

what if I got three rolls of paper towel and spilled something
after my third roll of paper towel ran out and if I had only gotten two rolls of paper towel I would have run out of paper towel
earlier and would have gone to get two more rolls of paper
towel before this happened and would be well stocked in paper
towel by the time the spill came around and
really what I am thinking is maybe

if I choose the right choice here and now in the paper towel aisle
of the grocery store then my life is going to change and that

this one small choice will butterfly effect itself into
finally
some new life because
isn't that what we are always told that every small action counts
that one small thing can change someone's life and so how are we
not always folding under the pressure of EVERY SMALL
THING MATTERING IN THE BIGGEST WAYS AND

SO NOTHING IS EVER REALLY A SMALL THING
IS IT NOT
EVEN HOW MANY ROLLS OF PAPER TOWEL TO
GET AND NOW I AM
in a different store and I have
found a shirt I love but
it fits me in two different sizes and

if a shirt fits in two different sizes should I just

get both and wear the larger shirt in contexts where the larger
shirt would be better and the smaller shirt in contexts where the
smaller shirt would be better and I
wish there was no choice at all but now I am

thinking

□ □

even if there was just the shirt in one size
should I buy two identical versions of it because
why would I not want a backup of a shirt that I found that I
adore because
do you even understand how hard it is to find a shirt that I love
and
what would I do if something happened to it like

⊡ □

if I tore it or

⊡ □

it slowly shrinks in the wash

▫ □

which is incidentally another reason to get the larger shirt and
what if

⬇

I spilled something on it and

▼

why do I have this preoccupation with spilling I don't

think I've spilled anything in years because

one of the upsides of worrying about spilling things is that you're
generally pretty careful about not spilling anything BUT

THE MOMENT YOU LET YOUR GUARD DOWN IS
ALWAYS WHEN IT HAPPENS AND WHAT IF
THE ONE TIME IT HAPPENS IS WHEN I HAVE

an important job interview or I have

an important meeting or it's just

on a day where I have to interact with any person at all or I am

just at home by myself and even in that situation it

means I have ruined my shirt and then I think
so what happens if my shirt gets destroyed and I
don't have that shirt anymore
well I can always get it again but then
what if I look up the shirt and I
find that

the store no longer sells that specific shirt anymore or

THE STORE NO LONGER EXISTS ANYMORE
BECAUSE AFTER ALL
EVERYTHING IS CLOSING THESE DAYS SO

why would I not stockpile as many of this one favorite shirt as I
possibly can before it disappears but even
if I do that which of the two sizes should I get or should I just

get a bunch of both sizes so I can decide later and HOW

are there One Thousand different choices of yogurt and I don't
even know if I want yogurt but now I'm
looking at all the kinds of yogurt because now I'm in front of the
milk and dairy wall and now I feel
like I have to decide because

there is a DECISION TO BE MADE AND I AM

GOING TO MAKE THE RIGHT ONE BECAUSE THIS
YOGURT IS GOING TO CHANGE MY LIFE WHEN I
DECIDE WHICH ONE IT IS AND I

don't know where to begin should I

look at the sugar content first or decide if I

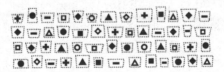

want fruit on the bottom or

maybe just start with choosing the flavor first but
what if the flavor I choose doesn't come in the yogurt-type I want
or what if my dad was right and that I should only get fat-free
yogurt or maybe
whole milk will have a richer flavor and make me Happier and
what is

"AUSTRALIAN-STYLE" or

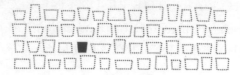

what if I get food poisoning if I choose the CONTAINER that
happens to have something bad in it and
it feels like there are too many variables and
it feels like I'm trying to decipher something that has One Thousand different translations and which of those could ever be the
right one so I
do what I always do in these situations which is I
text you and

? ↑

I ask for your opinion so it can override my inability to make my
own decision and so your opinion can become my decision but
really I
am just asking you so you will free me and maybe
it's because you are the only part of my life that never feels like a
decision that I am pressured to make but
it's also because I know

what you will say is what you always say which is
just choose any of them they're all good don't worry about it at all
and
even *don't worry about it at all* is a decision even if it's not the one
I was trying to make and
when you say it, it doesn't hurt or diminish my feelings and
when you say it, it is freeing and

when you say it, I realize that that decision was the one I was
trying to reach for on my own but I just couldn't

through all this information in front of me that I had to decipher
and

all this text in front of me that I had to translate but now

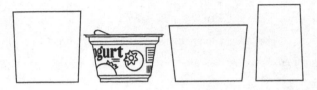

I am holding a Blueberry Flavored Whole Milk Greek Style Cup
of Yogurt, and now

I am putting it in my basket, and now

I am walking away from the dairy wall,

and all I can find myself thinking is,

   *it cannot be by coincidence that "decide" and "decode" are only
one letter apart.*

Anxiety tax

One way of coping with my anxiety has been to imagine it as a tax. In order to do the things I want to do, in order to go about my life, or to get anything done, I just need to pay the anxiety tax first. The tension and soreness I feel in my shoulders that never goes away; the hour of preparation it takes for me to talk myself into leaving the house; the constant fear that I will say the wrongest thing or write the wrongest thing or do the wrongest thing without even knowing it—these are all part of the tax.

I don't know if it's healthy, but at least it helps me separate my anxiety from myself. It's not who I am, it's not my personality, it doesn't represent me. It's just a tax I pay so that whoever I really am can go about his life.

Work friends

Something I've learned to tell myself about collaboration is that if I find people to work on something with at a time when we are all available and excited to work on something together, then I should drop everything and take the opportunity to work with them. That window may disappear tomorrow. Either they will get busy or I will or the motivation or inspiration or energy will disappear the next day. I have to do it now or it might be gone forever.

This particular anxiety, this desperation, I think is less about making the work—but more because it may be one of the only ways I know how to make friends. Working on something with someone who cares about making the same thing you do feels to me like the only real way to find someone who shares the same interests and the same passions as you do. And it gives us some easily followable roadmap toward friendship—there is no anxiety of what are we supposed to do with our time and are we using it well and what if we run out of things to talk about and Are We Having Fun Right Now I Think We're Having Fun Right

Now, because all we have to do is work on the project together, and talk about the project, and in that way, we are also hanging out, but with the bonus that we are also *Working*!

And in working together, I am not questioning what the other person is getting out of interacting with me at any given moment. If I am able to contribute my time, my energy, my attention, and my productivity to something, I am adding some tangible value to this friendship, right? I'm worth being friends with, right? I'm not wasting their time, right? And if they care about the work, and I am part of the working, by extension, doesn't that mean they care about me? And that I care about them?

Therapy friends

Perhaps there is one other way I feel like I know how to make friends.

I feel like I'm a good therapy friend.

A therapy friend is a friend who is an outsider to all of your circles of friends and to everyone else you know who listens to your problems (generally about everyone else you know, or about things that everyone else you know can't know that you worry about) and who you can confide in *because* they are an outsider. It's safe to tell them things because no one else you know knows them—so who are they going to tell? They are a secret-keeper, but really, in most cases, they don't even register that what you talk to them about are secrets to be kept because they don't know any of the people that these secrets need to be kept from. In healthy cases, therapy friendships are mutual—you confide in each other.

I believe it's healthy to have these secret-keepers, these external friends, who can just hear you out and give some sort of outside perspective to your life and everyone else who fills it.

My issue is, every time I talk to my therapist, I've started noting down what he does—the ways he responds to what I say, the kinds of questions he asks me—that make me feel validated and listened to. I do this in order to learn how to be a better therapy friend. And I think I've worked hard on being a nonjudgmental, supportive, and active listener to the extent that this is the only role of friendship I feel comfortable in. I am good at molding myself into being a listener that someone else wants around, who exists to provide support and affirmation. In this way, I can be . . . helpful, I guess? Or useful?

I do this, though, because it is another way to make me feel like I am adding value. I fear that without doing this form of work, maybe I, just as myself, am not worth the time or the attention or the friendship.

Three concepts for a birthday party

FIRST CONCEPT FOR A BIRTHDAY PARTY

Divide the pressure of one big party by the number of guests you are thinking of inviting, then meet each of those people separately over the course of the entire year for coffee, for lunch, for dinner, for a movie, spreading the single birthday party into a collection of smaller but no less revelatory moments, making each moment you share with a friend its own tiny celebration.

SECOND CONCEPT FOR A BIRTHDAY PARTY

Have a party and invite all the people you want to celebrate your existence with and try to enjoy it for once, just this one time. Don't think about how everyone you invite might be better friends with each other than any of them are with you, and don't think about how you might end up standing in the corner with nobody to talk to at your own party.

And definitely don't think about how you have no consistent version of yourself because you can only construct who you are in the context of another person, that you can only be "someone" by being who you think the other person would like to have around, so you are really no one when you are by yourself because you cannot be who you yourself would like to have around, and so there is no you, and instead please just be a normal person, one single normal person, not some Ungraspable Multitude, maybe just this once, on your own birthday, please. But whose birthday did all these people come to celebrate? Each of them came to celebrate a different person. So how can they all be at the same one party? And how can you be all these different people, all at once, all at the same time?

THIRD CONCEPT FOR A BIRTHDAY PARTY

Maybe just don't have a birthday party again this year, just like last year, just like every year, because you still don't know who it is you're supposed to be celebrating the existence of.

Ghost story

Hi, sorry, did you used to live on Hampshire Street?

This is what a message that appeared in my Message Requests tab on Facebook read, back when people used to check Facebook every three months or so in case they missed some important update from an older relative or a high school friend they hadn't spoken to in years, as opposed to nowadays, when people check Facebook never.

I responded. The person who sent this message had a photo of a dog as his profile picture, and for a second I entertained the idea that a dog had learned to type and learned to use Facebook for the sole purpose of sending me a Facebook message asking if I was the previous tenant of the basement-level—sorry, *Garden-Level*—apartment that the dog now lives in. I was in fact the previous tenant, but unfortunately the person who sent this message was not a Facebook-literate dog (which, honestly, was for the best anyway, as it is my personal belief that dogs do not need to be poisoned by Facebook memes), but just a regular, human person. And this human person had some of my mail, and we decided on a time for me to come by what was now *his* garden-level apartment to pick it up.

It's weird, walking up to a building you used to live in, that you used to call home but that you've now left behind. By the time you get buzzed in, and you make your way to the door that used to be your door, the feeling of being home overrides the knowledge that you don't live here anymore. It's strange knocking on your own door. This might have been the first and only time I'd knocked on this door before.

When I heard the deadbolt unlock for the split second before the door opened, I had this sudden sinking feeling in my chest. I was convinced that when the door opened, I would see that the person who had opened the door, who had been living in this apartment this whole time after I had moved out, was me. He would have my face and my hair and my glasses and would be wearing my clothes and then I'd look down at my own hands and there'd be no hands to look at, and no arms, and no body at all. I'd be thin air, and the me that opened the door would look out into the hallway, confused, then shrug and close the door and go back inside. And then I, the air, would diffuse into all of the rest of the air around me, and everything would go dark forever. Naturally.

Instead, something that felt even more strange than that happened, which was that the person who opened the door was not me, but a stranger, and I, standing in the hallway, was still me, solid and heavy and very strangely *not* still somehow living here.

"Jonathan? Here's your mail."

"Thank you! Hi!"

"See ya."

Then the door closed. I tried to say *wait*—I wanted to strike up a conversation. It felt like we were so linked—we both made the very personal choice to live in this place and I didn't under-

Croton

When a plant's leaves get soggy and wilted, or brown and dried up, my inclination is to keep them attached to the plant because I think, I hope, that those leaves will grow back and become green and healthy again. But this doesn't happen. I have been told that you must prune these unhealthy leaves because otherwise, they will just drain the plant of its resources, its energy, its life. I always worry that pruning these leaves will make the plant look empty, bare, noticeably missing something, and that it will leave the plant looking more unhealthy than it does with the dying leaves still attached. But as soon as you remove those leaves, all you see is what remains, which is a plant with green leaves, alive, and you forget about all the other leaves that were attached to it before.

stand why he wanted to end this exchange. All I wanted to do was look inside, to see how things had changed, see how he dealt with the lack of light fixtures, or the leaky window frames, or the gaps where the floor pulled down and away from the baseboard where the air and the bugs could get in. I felt that we'd have so much to talk about! We could share tips! Bond over the persistent damp coldness! The single-paned windows! And I could see if the dog in his Facebook profile picture liked the place! This was someone who was now making a home out of a place that I once made a home out of. I felt that we shared a connection through this place.

But to him, I was just some stranger named Jonathan. Maybe he saw the way I lived in it when he was being shown my apartment as a prospective tenant and thought *What a mess* and maybe at least he knew that much about me—which was much more than I knew about him. But even if he didn't see how I used to have a cardboard box as my nightstand, all I was to him was someone from the past who gave up this space, who forfeited any connection I had to it, so he could claim it as his.

As I left, I had the urge—which I did not act on—to go around to the parking lot in the back and crouch down with my knees on the asphalt and peek into my old, squat, *Garden-Level* windows along the ground and see how this new person was occupying *my* space. Did he gravitate toward the same corner that I did, or did he like the bad corner and not appreciate the good one? Did he throw his clothes in a pile in the same spot that I did—did he even *have* a semipermanent clothes pile spot at all? Did he orient his bed the same way that I did? Did he know about the power outlet that I only discovered when I moved out? And suddenly I understood hauntings. I was the ghost. And I didn't even have to die to become one, I just had to leave.

Particles

I think to get to the point where I can understand that I've changed, I have to dissociate from any past version of myself first. I have to treat those past versions of myself as outside of me, so I can see how I am different from those past selves.

But when I dissociate my past from my present too cleanly, when I don't acknowledge that I am still in some way, my past selves, I think that everything I've ever done has been done by a younger me who I no longer am, and everything I aspire to do needs to be done by an older me who I am not yet, and so present me is always doing, never having done, and never achieving anything. Present me is the most useless version of myself.

And I worry that I will feel this way at every point in my life.

What makes me feel a little better is telling myself that I am an older me to my past selves and a younger me to my future selves. And since present me is able to look at my past and future selves with some sort of admiration—that they are the ones who either *have accomplished* or *will accomplish*—it means that there are always people—my past selves and my future selves—who are looking at me like that, too. Sometimes this adds pressure—*I have to hold the expectations of not only myself but of all these other people now, too?? I'm not letting just myself down but letting all these versions of myselves down??*—but for the most part, it helps me to know that I have been and will be thought of with some sort of kindness when I can't muster that for myself right now. There are past versions of me who believe in me, and there are future versions of me who are looking back on where I am and thinking, *That's the version of me who actually managed to achieve something.* There are always these people cheering me on, or, at the very least, thinking about me. And that helps me feel less alone. And that helps me feel like I am right where I need to be.

Wave fact

One thing I have always remembered from physics class is a detail about the way a wave travels through a medium of particles. The wave travels laterally through the particles, creating a waveform, but the particles themselves just move up and down in place, each particle moving up then down, causing the next particle to move up then down, causing the next particle to move up then down, and so on, articulating the wave through their sequential displacement over time.

You can visualize this by imagining a rubber duck, floating in a still pond, with a ripple approaching it. When the ripple reaches the rubber duck, the rubber duck isn't taken along with the ripple—it just bobs up and down, letting the ripple pass under it, and stays more or less in place.

Now imagine a long line of rubber ducks, all floating in this pond, with a ripple approaching. As the ripple passes under each rubber duck, each of these rubber ducks does the same thing, bobbing up and down, but staying relatively in place, remaining more or less in line with all the other ducks.

Now imagine that the *entire surface of the pond* is covered with rubber ducks—you get the point. That one's just a fun thing to imagine.

Each of those rubber ducks acts the same way that a water particle does when a ripple moves across the water.

The water particle doesn't see the waveform at all. It just moves up and down following the particles before it.

And so it only looks like a wave to the observer, someone above the water, someone who is not a water particle themselves.

Sometimes I picture how my life might build in waves. For a wave to happen, Monday-me must move, then Tuesday-me must move, then Wednesday-me must move, and across all these movements, a wave may form over time.

I think perhaps what's so difficult about trying to witness our own changes is that we are not above the water. We are each just moving up and down in place, trying to stay afloat.

Addenda to Schrödinger's paradox

SCHRÖDINGER'S PARADOX

A man places a cat in a closed box with a radioactive atom and a vial of poisonous gas that is set up to a mechanism that detects the state of the atom such that if the atom decays, the vial of poisonous gas is shattered and the cat dies, but if the atom doesn't decay, the vial stays intact and the cat lives. Because the box is closed, the man cannot observe what has happened until he opens the box.

The Copenhagen interpretation of quantum superposition states that prior to being observed, the atom has no definitive properties and exists as a combination of all its possible states at once, *both* decayed *and* non-decayed *at the same time* until it is observed, at which point it collapses into a single state, which is the state that it is observed as.

Therefore, until the man opens the box to observe the state

of the atom through what happens to the cat, the atom is *both* decayed—and therefore the vial has been shattered and the cat is dead—*and* non-decayed—and therefore the vial has remained intact and the cat is alive. Therefore, before the box is opened and before the man observes what has happened, when the atom is in both a decayed and a non-decayed state at the same time, is the cat dead, or is the cat alive?

ADDENDA TO SCHRÖDINGER'S PARADOX

When the cat sits inside the box, in the dark, do they know if they are dead or alive at any given point, or do they only know when this man who has claimed authority over the cat's state, who has claimed authority as the objective observer opens the box and tells them what they are?

When the box is opened and the man declares, for every reality where the cat still lives, *"Alive!"* does the cat know what *"Alive!"* means?

And does the cat think, then, having never been declared *"Dead!"* that *"Dead!"* is every other moment where the man has not declared that the cat is *"Alive!"* or does the cat believe that they have never been *"Dead!"* at all?

When the man opens the box, does the cat aspire to be told, once again, that they are *"Alive!,"* or does the cat aspire to, just one of these times, because it hasn't happened yet, be told that it is finally dead?

When the cat is not in the box, when they are of no use to the man as he thinks of other experiments to conduct, does the cat find any fulfillment in simply being a cat? Or do they spend their every waking moment waiting to get back into the box, to be part of something they have been told all their life is more important than themself?

When the man dies, does the cat believe it? Does the cat think, if the man were truly dead, why didn't the man himself declare to the cat that he was?

When the man dies, does the cat still belong to the man?

When the man dies, does the cat feel free?

When the cat steps outside the laboratory afterward and finds other cats who have never been told that they are alive and who do not know what *"Alive!"* is, does the cat feel *more* alive, with the authority of having been told that they are, or do they feel far less so, knowing that, to these other cats, *"Alive!"* doesn't mean anything at all?

Without the man to tell them so, does the cat worry that they will never know what state they are in again? Or can the cat learn to declare for themself their own state?

When the cat meets another cat who can observe them, can the cat be comfortable with simply knowing they are observed, or do they constantly feel the urge to scream, *"TELL ME! AM I DEAD? AM I ALIVE?"*

And does the other cat answer? Does the other cat know how to?

And if the cat has kittens—if the cat should want to have kittens, and if the cat does have kittens—can the cat allow the kittens to simply exist as they are, in the state that they are in? Or does the cat hold their kittens a little too tightly, for a little too long, whispering into their little kitten ears until it drowns out their own thoughts, *"you're alive, you're alive, you're alive"*?

Part 4: Hello

What if instead of working anymore I just walked straight into the ocean

. . . went for a nice refreshing swim, created some space for impossible problems to loosen and untangle in the background, reorganized my priorities, and reoriented where I share my time and give my attention?

Sunlight

I've started to take more breaks, or rather, Elissa has started forcing me to take more breaks, because I keep burning myself out. And of all the break-taking we do together, I've come to enjoy being around nature the most.

Taking the time to be around nature is helping me understand that things can just exist, being what they are, and it's just each of us that gives them some sort of meaning.

The sun is just the sun. A tree just grows because the conditions are right for it to do so.

But when we come across a moment where the daylight isn't everywhere, where the trees block out most of the sky, and the sun shines on a smattering of leaves, or a small wildflower, or a patch of moss, it feels like it's highlighting it just for us.

Here, the sun is no longer just the sun. It leaks through the trees and becomes a spotlight.

Prayer plant

I used to think that plants were static, pointless things. But once I started bringing them into my home and started taking care of them, watering them the way they like, giving them the right soil, placing them in the right light, I began to notice that they would move. I started noticing that they would grow toward their closest window, reaching for the light. I started seeing them slowly will new leaves into existence and will old leaves out of existence. I started to see how they were alive.

Elissa picked out a prayer plant for us once that moved more than any other plant I've ever seen.

It had deep green leaves with bright pink veins that looked like they were painted on, as if they were asking for us to notice them, to pay attention to how their positions in the day were different than how they positioned themselves at night.

Every night, the leaves would point straight up, clustering together as if the plant was closing itself in, guarding itself from the world, to face inward and reflect on the day.

Every morning, we would find the plant had opened up, leaves facing out into the world, taking in the new day with excitement and welcome. Every morning, I looked forward to waking up and seeing it had already become open, and every evening, I looked forward to glancing over at it and noticing that at some point, it had already closed up and said good night. Its movements were so minute that it was impossible to see it move by simply watching it, but sure enough, every night it would be closed up, and every morning it would be open, so there was definitive proof that it was in fact moving, even if we could not observe its motion ourselves. It helped me become excited for each new day—I wanted to catch the plant taking just one day off, to either stay closed during the day, or stay open over the night, but it never did. It lived a structured, disciplined life.

The act of taking care of plants, every day, over the courses of months and years, has helped show me that life takes time, but with time, life, for the most part, seems to generally know what to do.

And learning when to provide the right pieces and how to set the right variables and conditions makes you a part of that life, too.

You take care of the plant, and, if the plant decides to stay alive, it shows you how you are part of things outside of yourself, how you are more than yourself.

Sometimes, it shows you a new leaf, slowly, slowly emerging out of a plant you care for, unfurling and growing until you can't tell it is the new one anymore.

I may have helped that leaf come into existence, but really, the plant is what did the growing. And here, the plant helps me in return. It helps me understand that, over the course of its own growing, I must have grown, slowly unfurling in some way or another, too.

Taking care of these plants and noticing those small growths become big growths that allow for more new small growths to happen has made me appreciate that they, like ourselves, like all things, require time. Plants change and grow on a scale of weeks, months, years. You don't notice how alive they are in a glance, but when you notice that they move, and when you notice that they have grown, it's a sudden thrill. Every plant is an explosion of life, except that to us, they burst forth in slow motion.

To the plants, though, we must be exhausting. Being around any plants at all makes me imagine them witnessing me moving around all the time, a fast-forwarded blur of sitting, standing, sitting, laying down, sitting, standing, sitting, standing, sitting, until the plant gives up, sighing, burned-out, *Enough with this guy already. Stop moving around so much. Just sit still for a couple weeks. Please.*

Even when our prayer plant started dying, when I would fail to keep it alive, each leaf furling and turning crisp then falling

off, it would still welcome every day with the opening of its remaining leaves, and would still say good night by closing up with
what it had left.

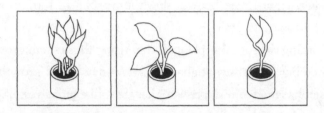

Eventually, the plant became just one single leaf, a symbol of my
own failings to keep it alive, and still, this one leaf would bend
forward every morning, now looking less like an opening up but
more like a bowing down, gracious for the light, grateful to still
be here for another day.

And at night, it would stand up, stoic, waiting—or hoping—it
would live long enough to get to see the sun again.

When the plants I care for grow, it feels like they are teaching me to experience my own happiness in slow motion, over the course of weeks, months. And when they die, when they start to dry out, or wilt, or rot at the root, they die slowly, too. Earlier in my life, I had avoided the plants that were dying slow deaths by throwing them in the compost prematurely, as soon as they showed signs that they might not be able to be saved. But even in the slow sadness of a dying plant, I have now come to appreciate that there is something peaceful about how slowly that panic and hopelessness and frustration and guilt unfurls, every morning and every night, over and over again, and how slowly the plant teaches me to feel it, to accept it, until one day it cannot teach me anything, anymore.

On drawing and drawing plants

A simple fact about me: basically any drawing of a plant is going to fill me with awe. I can't help it. I'm a simple person . . . I see a drawing of a plant and I feel elated.

Any drawing is—it must be—a portrait of the person who drew it. It is a personal statement, because it's about what they've chosen to put onto paper. It's a portrait in first-person, through what they've noticed and how they see.

One piece of drawing advice that has always stuck with me is just "draw what you notice." That can be a high density of specific details, or it can be a single curious line, or an unusual curve. It can also be what isn't there at all—what has been intentionally omitted that might have felt necessary to be included by somebody else. All of this is what makes your drawing yours. To draw is to visually manifest one's attention and care. And the drawing is simultaneously the *result* and the *proof* of that caring. It is a product made of attention and made of time.

A plant, too, is a result and a proof of time and attention.

This is why any drawing of a plant is so compelling to me.

It is something that takes time (the drawing) *of* something that takes time (the plant).

When I draw my plants, the act of drawing helps me take the time to notice the details of something that I have given my time to take care of. It helps me appreciate that I am able to give my attention consistently and over a long period. And ultimately, I suppose, I like having the drawing as proof, as some sort of paper receipt showing that I've given all that time and attention to what I'm drawing rather than letting all that time and attention simply collect in the subject itself.

Fittonia

When I started getting into houseplants, I bought a Fittonia along with a pothos and a Janet Craig plant (Who was Janet Craig? And why did she have this plant named after her? And how do I get a plant named after me?) because I was told by the person selling them to me that they were all supposed to be very easy to care for.

The Janet Craig plant was the easiest to care for but the least satisfying because no matter how much or how little I watered it, it seemed to never change or move at all, and its passage through time was only marked with little tender blades appearing out from its center that I was surprised to notice one day, but that did not appear to grow at all in the months following their seemingly sudden appearance.

The pothos was also easy to care for, needing little light and being forgiving with waterings, and it was satisfying because when watered regularly, it would grow quickly, leaves unfurling over days, vines growing over weeks, and it would move a little, too, its stems getting firm and leaves raised toward its nearest window after being watered.

The Fittonia, however, worried me because it did not seem easy to care for at all. It seemed fragile and sensitive to waterings and would threaten to die whenever it was not getting enough water or sunlight or humidity or heat or attention. One day it would be totally fine, but the next, every single one of its leaves would look, somehow, both dried out and wilted at the same time, as if every leaf agreed to put on this show all at once so that I would notice it.

There was a period when I had neglected to water all three of these plants for about a week because my focus was drawn to a deadline so I had cleared from my mind everything that wasn't related to the deadline, and while the other two plants barely reacted to not being watered, the Fittonia drooped dramatically, leaves wilting over the edges of the pot, limbs lying entirely life- less, like a deep sigh, asking for me to notice it.

The first time this happened, I thought it was definitely on its way to dead and would be impossible to nurture back, but I wa- tered it anyway, just out of some naive hope, and within minutes of me giving it my attention, it perked right up, firm and crisp and tall as if nothing had ever happened.

On attention

One thing that has made me less anxious about talking to people is focusing on this notion that a conversation is a gift of somebody's time and attention. The person you're talking with decided in that moment that you are more important than everything else they have going on, and they chose you—and you chose them—to spend some amount of time with. That used to cause me a great deal of stress, because I'd worry that I wasn't worth the time or the attention, but lately I have been recalling how excited I feel when I want to share my time and attention with someone and am imagining that the other person might be feeling some version of that toward me as well. I bring my time and attention, and they bring their time and attention, and we are both hoping that if the conditions are good—or good enough—that something will know how to grow out of it, and that makes me feel a little better about it all.

On presence

I have a friend who, in my opinion, is truly great at texting. Speaking to someone through text requires its own cues to show presence. And when texting, I find myself wondering what the equivalent of eye contact is, to the extent that there can be one, or what the equivalent of active listening is.

I think what makes my friend great at texting is that when we are locked into a text conversation, it feels like they are truly present. There is no delay time lasting minutes or hours while we wait to get back to each other. It feels like a direct back-and-forth. I send a text (or a series of texts), I see the ellipses cycle as they immediately start to type, I see their text (or series of texts), I immediately start typing my response, and so on.

For me, active listening through texting, in one sense, happens when I see the other person typing, and so I stop typing—so that my message doesn't interrupt what the next thing is that they are going to say. That way, I feel as if I am yielding the floor to them, allowing their message to be the focus and to guide what comes next in the conversation. And I feel like my friend reciprocates this too. While we are in conversation, each of our brief silences while the other is texting isn't representative of absence but of attention.

And when this friend who is great at texting has to go, they say so: "Sorry, I have to go into a meeting now" or "I'm going to make dinner now" or simply "I have to go now!" There's such a clear delineation between when they are sharing their attention with me and when they are not, so that when they are, it feels active, and present, and focused.

On proof

It was in high school that I started to notice my anxiety deepen. I had always been quiet, but I was becoming more and more aware of how certain situations, such as speaking to people or being around people, filled me with uncertainty and made me sweat and sometimes made me want to throw up. I would plan out conversations in my head and try to prepare how I would say hello to someone, and come up with a list of topics to talk about that might interest the person I was planning to talk to, and think of what I could say that might be funny or interesting about those topics. And if I actually managed to get as far as talking to that person, and if I actually managed to hang on to the conversation for long enough that it started going into unplanned territory, toward a new topic I hadn't planned for, or sticking deeper to the same topic but beyond what I had planned on saying—in other words, if a conversation started developing organically, the way that conversations do when they are going well and the conditions for them to grow are good—I would feel naked, and unprepared, and I would get so nervous about accidentally saying the wrong thing that would cause the conversation to end, that I would end the conversation as quickly as I could to prevent that from happening, which would just cause the thing I feared—that the conversation would end—to happen anyway. But at least it felt like a more controlled demolition this way. And as I would walk away, I would play out the conversation over and over in my head to figure out what had brought us to this point that I had not prepared for, and I would try to figure out what I should have said in the moment, coming up with a new list of things to say so I wouldn't be caught off guard if this topic ever came up again. It felt like I had a problem with processing time—that on the spot, I couldn't think fast enough, I didn't have time to safely plan out what I wanted to say before I could say it, and I would panic and say nothing at all, or stumble to get any coherent words out in any coherent sense of order as any coherent thought.

In high school, everyone was also talking through instant messaging. My school's platform for this was MSN Messenger. And through MSN, talking to people felt . . . easier. I felt like the way I typed on MSN was truer to the ways I always imagined I could speak that I held in my head. Knowing that I had at least a few seconds to respond, that there was that accepted lag time between responses, gave me the ability to properly choose my words and plan out what I wanted to say, in the way I wanted to say it. And with that, I felt like I could more accurately communicate the way that I always knew that I could, and through this, I was able to be smart, funny, thoughtful, interesting.

This is where I learned to speak, really.

When a friend from school who I rarely ever talked to in person but did all the time on MSN went away to camp for the summer, we wrote each other letters. I got really good at writing letters. I loved sitting down and taking the time to write them and ending up with pages and pages to show for it, and I loved reading the letters that they sent back to me, knowing they took the time to write to me, too. In reading them, it felt like I was holding their time in my hands.

When school came back in the fall, the closeness we gained through exchanging letters all summer somehow didn't translate when we would talk in person. Whenever we talked in person, it felt like we could never reach the same highs as we did when we would write to each other, and that I could never live up to being as funny and thoughtful and articulate as I could when I was writing. And so I think, without ever talking about it, we both somehow agreed upon an unspoken mutual pact to kind of just avoid each other at school so we wouldn't have to be forced to talk to each other in person. But after school every day, we'd still get back on MSN and message each other for hours and have great conversations long into every evening.

Even though this desire to talk online came originally from being anxious about speaking out loud, there was something new, something different about communicating through text that I was drawn to, too. There were so many ways to convey meaning and tone and emotion through text, and with a higher level of control and ability, so I could get things right and accurately say what I wanted and meant to say. I knew how to finally convey all these elements of myself that I knew I was made up of, now that my in-person failures didn't get in my own way of me being funny, attentive, caring, thoughtful.

On MSN, everyone seemed to operate on the same unspoken but very specific and real rules of how to talk to each other through text. And these rules were the first rules of communication in any form that I felt like I really knew my way around. I knew that different ways of writing out text—in all lowercase, in all uppercase, in proper sentence case—all meant something different. I knew that if you sent a bunch of short, one-word messages all in a row, it meant something different than sending one long paragraph all as one message. I knew what all the emoticons meant, and I knew how each of them could be used to convey the very specific feelings that you couldn't as effectively convey through words, and that I didn't know how to convey in person. I knew that ending a message with a period meant something different than ending it with a single exclamation mark or multiple exclamation marks or an ellipsis or no punctuation at all. I knew that ending a question with a single question mark felt way too serious or accusatory or patronizing because that made the question feel like homework, so I never did that. All of this felt so much more decipherable and legible, so much easier to decode and to use to accurately convey meaning and tone than the in-person elements of my face, my body, my voice, which felt entirely impossible to wield with any sense of control or precision or accuracy at all.

And I was drawn to how presence was so much more legible online—that if someone was talking to you, it was because they wanted to—otherwise, they could just appear offline to you or not respond back so quickly and then later make up an excuse like, "Sorry, I was away from my computer," or "Sorry, I was doing homework." In person, I always felt that I was bothering people, interrupting their lives and their days and their routines with my presence, and that they couldn't politely get away so they had to talk to me.

In person, too, conversations felt so intangible. They disappear after they happen so they leave nothing behind to show for them. We have our memories of them, but I was always left with this fear that I had remembered a conversation with someone so differently than the other person had.

On MSN, though, there was proof the conversation happened—it was written down! If I forgot what someone said, or if I was worried that someone didn't like me, I could just scroll up and look at all the words we wrote out to each other and find comfort in having some sort of tangible evidence that we had given all this time and attention to each other previously.

Even better, we were writing down our funniest moments, our best jokes, our deepest and wisest observations, our attention and our friendship and our secrets and our joy as we were speaking them. When I spoke with someone on MSN, it felt, somehow, more real, because we were committing it to text.

And even though I never went back and read them, I took comfort in knowing that the MSN extension I had installed called *Messenger Plus! by Patchou* that had allowed me to format my text differently and use custom status tags and set up auto replies when I was away from my keyboard had *also* had a feature that saved the chat logs of all my MSN conversations into text files in a folder on my computer. And I loved knowing that in some folder, the act of talking to a friend was filling a .txt document with thousands and thousands of words. That by talking, we were writing a novel, or a script, or something even more. And that made it feel like what we were doing was much more than just talking. In writing all these words together, over years and years, it felt like we were collaborating, like we had written a friendship into being.

A waste of time and energy

When you walk into the Rehearsal Factory in Toronto, you are immediately immersed in the sounds behind every door of every rehearsal room in the building. The sounds present themselves all at once, but keep themselves distinct, never blending into a gray mush but instead folding into and out of each other like a kaleidoscope, sixteen rooms making sixteen fragments that add up to something that isn't just a whole, but sounds like a curated collection of every sound that has ever been played in the building. If you're lucky, your rehearsal room is on the third floor, and as you climb the service stairs up from the entrance on the first floor, past rooms 1–8 on the second floor, and then up to rooms 9–16 on the third, the sounds from each floor reach out into the stairwell and you become part of each band rehearsing in the space, you become part of each group of kids learning to play together by practicing covers of someone else's songs, you become part of each group of touring musicians who drove to Toronto in the morning and are running their set before they are to perform in the evening, you become part of the young artists working through new material, you become part of all of it because for a brief moment, you are a part of what they are doing—you are their only audience, their only witness to the sound they are making outside of themselves. If you're me, you are here to become part of a group of old friends, getting together to create music that did not exist before tonight and is never meant to be played a second time.

When you leave the Rehearsal Factory, you don't really hear the sounds from all the other rooms—when you leave, you leave with yourself, with your band, filled with the sounds you and your friends created that you witnessed being plucked out of thin air, which then diffuse back into the air as soon as they become heard. When you leave, you leave with your ears ringing, saturated, unable to take in any more sound from any other room that you pass, even though the thin doors adorned with metal numbers do very little to keep the sound being made in each of these rooms from spilling out.

The fact that the doors, and the walls for that matter, in the Rehearsal Factory aren't soundproof makes it, on paper, a terrible rehearsal space. But it makes it a perfect place to create music spontaneously. It's a perfect place to feel like you're at the heart of something, to feel tapped in like a lightning rod, or a medium, channeling whatever you've been going through and whatever is going on around you. Luckily, that's what we're here to do, to grab at whatever we can find, whatever we've brought in with us, as we try to come up with something together, anything, as time moves forward to a beat that Ray, who plays the drums, keeps steady, at first, then on a whim, when he gets bored, turns unsteady, flowing into different tempos, different time signatures. This, too, the way he makes time explicit and ever changing, forces us to adapt, to keep up, to use whatever we have at our disposal and turn it into our own ways to make time sound.

The Rehearsal Factory used to be an apartment building, I think. Or maybe an office building. It certainly wasn't a factory before this, though the idea of naming a rehearsal space a rehearsal "Factory" makes me think of how this place too is—or wants to be—a place of work. Because the walls are thin, even when you're in your own rehearsal room, you can hear the intruding sound coming in from the left, right, and above (if you're on the second floor) or below (if you're on the third floor). The walls are draped with curtains—dark curtains, not soundproof curtains, but curtains dark enough to give off the appearance that they are meant to keep the sound out, or perhaps to assure you that they will keep the sound you make in.

I only started coming to the Rehearsal Factory after I moved away from Toronto, almost a decade ago now. My only relationship to it is as a place I go whenever I am back in town to visit, touching down for a few days, before I leave again.

Every time I visit, I try to text the jazz friends I used to play music with and arrange to meet here and kind of just free associate for a few hours. It feels like I'm Getting The Band Back Together. Never mind that The Band, aside from me, has been playing together regularly the entire time since I've moved away, and that I am the only person who is doing the Getting Back.

Ryan, who plays the bass, always coordinates booking the room. Ray plays the drums. Marc plays the keyboard and always brings his own laptop with all his custom sounds and effects, because these are the ones he knows how to use and can call up immediately when someone calls out a style to make up something in: *80s synth*! Or *church organ*! Or just a nice, muted piano. Every time we play, he always seems to have a new effect that he wants to experiment with and show us. Whenever Kevin is in town, he plays the guitar, and if he isn't around, we see if Jeff is free. I'll bring a case of beer and come up with some words. I spend most of my life now writing things down in ways to keep them permanent, so it's a welcome departure to spend these nights in the Rehearsal Factory writing only by speaking out whatever words come as soon as they come. Nothing on paper, nothing prepared beforehand. This amounts to something closer to a story or an essay or a monologue set to a soundtrack than to rap freestyle. The act of this used to be terrifying, but over time, this practice of speaking out loud whatever comes to mind, as it comes, scored to whatever music comes to the minds of my friends, has become freeing. And it has only become freeing because I have been doing this with this group of people who I trust and who I have learned to feel safe around. The thing that I have been rehearsing most, perhaps, is how to conjure this feeling of safety, of comfort, of trust.

The group shifts a little each time. There is the core group of Ryan, Ray, Marc, and Kevin/Jeff, but around them, we invite any of our other music friends who are available to come and join. I always try to talk my brother into coming, and when he does, he brings himself, and sings. When Amanda is free, she has a wonderful way of complementing and elevating every instrument with her voice. Kevin (another Kevin), my best friend and a Professional Actor In Theatre And Film, commands focus when he comes, crooning catchy silky nonsense. His husband, Danny, only ever comes to listen and cannot be convinced to sing, even though he used to do musical theater and we have all heard him sing and he is a beautiful singer.

None of us make a living by playing music. The jazz combo plays gigs here and there, but they also work day jobs—the gigs feel more like an excuse for them to play music together than anything else. I write. My brother is a student. None of us have come here to rehearse anything, and so it feels like we are not using the "Factory" in the right way. There is no "productive" outcome to this—no show, no album, no project we are working toward. It confounds my dad, "It's a waste of time and energy! Why don't you do something productive instead?"

———

I cannot imagine a world where I do not spend my whole life working. Work is perhaps the closest thing to a universal language that I know. This constant, heavy pressure that I should always be working is in control of where I focus my life, who I spend my time with, what I spend my time on.

And I cannot imagine a freedom in no longer working because I cannot imagine a reality where I no longer need to work to survive.

And so there is perhaps some small freedom, then, or perhaps just a tiny bit of relief, in directing our time and energy to something that we ourselves choose to do, with people we choose to be with.

And when I'm in Toronto, that looks like my friends and I getting together at the Rehearsal Factory. For hours, in the room that Ryan books that's hopefully on the third floor, we make music out of, and back into, thin air. It's just us, with no audience aside from, perhaps, the witnesses passing by our room on the way to their own rehearsals, and the listeners in the rooms around ours, making their own music that blends its way into everything we play. I'll shout in the dark, "Let's do something joyous, celebratory," and my friends will throw things around then throw them out for a few minutes until some of those things settle into something that sounds like maybe we could have heard it our entire lives. And I'll try to speak words into all its corners and pockets that make me believe that I've always known this song they're playing. And when we're out of ideas for it, we'll kind of all just come to an unspoken agreement to bring the song to an end, and we'll sit a bit in the silence, and maybe talk and catch up a little, and then someone else will throw some new idea into the air and we'll build a new song out of that.

And we'll do this over and over again, until our three hours of time that we've booked the rehearsal space for are up, which always feels like exactly the amount of time it takes for us all to get exhausted and burned out and happy from making up new things together. And then we leave, fulfilled and tired and hungry, and we walk until we get to someone's streetcar stop, then someone's subway stop, and slowly we fall away from each other, once again, like after the last time we did this.

Every time this is over, I always think to myself that we could have far more easily done nothing and then I wonder what compels us to keep doing this.

Sometimes, on our walk out into the cold—it feels like all my memories of Toronto are set in the winter—one of us will joke, "So when's our album coming out?" and I'll admit that I couldn't completely let our time go to waste, and I'll say, "Oh, well I recorded everything on my phone" and I'll go home and send the recordings to everyone, and we'll each listen to a few tracks of us slowly figuring out what the song is, slowly building it into a chorus and a verse and a hook, imperfect, but perhaps not imperfect at all because perfect was not the goal to begin with.

And I think about the promise of turning this into an album. And I feel confident, and maybe encouraged, by the fact that it will probably never happen, partly because we are each so busy with our own lives that we don't have the time to sort through all of this, but mainly, I think, because the joy that comes from doing this is in actively throwing away—and in celebrating the throwing away of—the work. In letting it disappear back into the air.

Or, because I am not brave enough to actually fully do that, to record everything on my phone just as proof that it happened, but to never do anything with it at all.

I used to dream that I could play in a band with all these friends, that we would write an album, that we would record it and maybe perform it in a few venues. And then I moved away, and I tried to find other people to play music with in the new cities I landed in but it just never happened, it never clicked, and eventually I was away from my friends for long enough and enough time had passed that I just had to let that dream go. Because while I held on to that dream, I couldn't be around music at all. The longing that it would bring up to make music with my friends who I was too far away from for too long was too much to bear. But now, after having let the dream go, I am able to find joy in revisiting some version of it, only now the dream just looks like playing music together whenever we can, once or twice a year if we're lucky, without any goal aside from simply being able to do it. I wonder if this is a compromise—some admission of defeat or some acknowledgment that we never achieved this dream—or if it is, in some way, a purer form of it. I wonder if I am simply keeping some old memory alive, trying to revisit some old glue from a time when we used to play all the time, or if this is something else. I wonder if maybe I am not trying to relive some lost dream but perhaps mourning it, celebrating it, and moving toward something new, instead.

I think a lot of pressure gets put on making things "for something" or "for some reason" and the pressure of "but *why?*" and "but who's this *for?*" and "is it good enough?" and "it's a waste of time and energy!" and "why don't you do something productive instead?" and I think that all of this removes the importance and value of making things for the ones who are making it, because maybe the ones who are making the thing are the ones who might need it the most.

And when I am back in town, and when we get together, what it feels like we are saying is that if we're going to put in the effort to work on something together, it's going to be for us, and only us, and for no one else, and in doing so, we can escape the pressures of needing a reason for just a little while.

Part 5: Hello, Again

Pothos

I read that pothos plants are able to thrive in pretty low light, so I kept ours in the back corner of our apartment, far from the window.

I watered it regularly and it grew and grew and seemed to be totally healthy and unbothered by its low light situation so I was happy that what I had read was right, except that after a few weeks of sitting in this corner, I noticed that the plant was growing quite lopsidedly toward the window, leaves reaching, aching, toward the light.

It looked unbalanced only growing to one side, and because I couldn't move the window to the other side of the plant, I rotated the pot so that the other side of the plant would face the window.

Elissa said to stop messing with it, that moving it around would disturb the plant, but I thought that it began to look better after a few weeks in its new orientation. It was a bit more balanced, its leaves now reaching out to the window on its other side, too.

The only thing that seemed unbalanced now was that the limbs that were originally reaching out to the window seemed to notice that they were no longer facing the window, and so they had turned around, reaching for the light that was now behind them.

As the limbs of the pothos grew longer and longer, their reaching, their yearning, got more noticeable.

One afternoon, this made me finally feel guilty enough for keeping the plant in its dark, perfectly fine, low-lit corner that I moved it right up to the window, placing it directly into the light, so it could have what it was reaching asking for.

A few days later, its leaves started to turn pale and brown—it had burned in the sun.

On finding ways to remember

Whenever I come home to visit, my mom takes all these photos of me, as proof, I imagine, that I still exist. As proof that I am older now. As proof that I was in this house, so when I leave again, she can show herself I was once there.

And I will stand in the doorway, saying, "You can just say hi, you've taken like fifty pictures, I think that's enough, can I come in now?" while she ignores everything I say and tells me to smile more, but don't smile too fake, smile naturally, not so big, control your smile, you should practice how you look when you smile, don't smile with your teeth so much, straighten your back, don't *gong ge yao*, don't play with your hands, fix your hair, don't *zhou mei tou*, all to get some frozen, lasting image to assign to and to overwrite, perhaps, an ephemeral, already fading memory.

Even though I complain, the truth is that I am comforted by the fact that there is proof that I came home to visit, too. Because I will be gone again before I know it.

Removing

One difficult feeling to fight when I am preparing to leave a place I love is the one that says that once I do, everyone will be totally fine without me, that everything will go on as if I hadn't existed at all, that I am not a necessary part of whatever the place is, that I can just slip away before the party ends and no one will even realize that I'm gone.

And when I do leave, when I move away, the hard part is understanding that this feeling wasn't just some hypothetical. When I leave, it becomes something that simply happens. People will go on with their lives. That place you were a part of, that you are now just some visitor to, will continue operating in your absence, will continue picking up more visitors, will continue to continue. It must.

And every time I return to visit, I see that it's true. My friends who stayed made new friends, or became better friends with my friends who also stayed. The places I was once part of kept going on without me. And the things that did close down, or end, or stop, did not do so *because* I left. It was just that they left *as well*, independent of anything to do with me. When I come back to visit, I see how so little was affected at all by my leaving.

The selfish part of all this is that I want to be important—I want to be *so* important that the world here falls apart, stops functioning, after I step out of it. And of course this doesn't happen. But there's a part of me that tells myself that if I were important, if I were *truly* important, my leaving would have had an impact. It would have done something. There would have been a hole that I left behind that people would notice. Instead, everything just keeps going on without me. And it feels like the lesson is, *you don't matter.*

But of course any act of leaving creates that hole. Every act of moving is also an act of removing, leaving an empty space where what moved is no longer there. It's just, the problem with leaving is that you're never able to stick around to see what you've left behind.

On the emptiness created by people you barely know

When people you barely know—the people who are not close to you and who you are not close to—disappear from your life, they leave a hole where there wasn't anything before. It's more harrowing, in some ways, than when someone close to you leaves, because when a stranger leaves, they don't even leave memories or stories or anything else behind for you. They just leave behind the hole. Their presence did not reveal a life to you, but their absence reveals a loss.

Whenever this happens, it reminds me that I wasn't paying enough attention to the people who vanish from my life this way—that I was considering them not as a full person, but as some background detail to my life, and now that they are gone, it just feels like some part of the set is missing.

The owner (who was also the chef) of the dumpling place my parents liked, who was always so friendly and close and gregarious with my parents, who was always excited to see me and my brother and would always comment on how much we grew, or how tall we were (I am, for the record, very averagely heighted), vanished from our lives this way, because the restaurant closed and my mom doesn't know what happened to her.

"Where did the restaurant go?" "It just closed one day." "So where do you go for dumplings now?" "Another place. It's almost as good." "Well do you have any way of getting in touch with her?" "We didn't even know her last name."

Then I ask my mom if that makes her sad, and she pauses for a second and then says, "That's just how things go."

On mourning

Mourning does not only apply to death. You are allowed to mourn change, as well. You can mourn an old home that is gone, or a world around you that has shifted so imperceptibly until one day it no longer feels familiar anymore.

You can mourn your own changes, too. That you are no longer the person you used to be is, in my opinion, a good reason for mourning. It may be a cause for celebration, sometimes, too. But you can always give who you once were a send-off, a memorial, before you move on from them.

Playlist for a funeral

I don't actively think about dying (or is it more accurate to say "I don't think about *actively* dying"?), but I do keep a list of songs that I think would sound nice to be playing in the background when I do. Like a soundtrack, or a list of possible songs to play when the credits roll, or maybe it's just a list of songs that I think would be okay to be the last song I ever hear before I go.

Perhaps more accurately, these songs make up a playlist that I would like to be playing after I am gone, during my funeral. Whatever this playlist is, it feels different to me than having a list of my *favorite* songs.

My ideal party, I think, would involve finalizing this list and then having my closest friends over to listen to it. Or maybe, rather, I'd have my closest friends over for an unrelated, very normal reason that I can't think of at the moment because I've never thrown a party for myself, and just have that playlist playing in the background, without anyone knowing that it is the playlist for my funeral. I can imagine all my closest friends enjoying themselves, talking and laughing, and we are celebrating some normal thing that people throw parties in celebration of, and I would finally be enjoying myself too, and I would be relaxed, and happy, because I would know that in the background, my funeral playlist is playing.

My funeral playlist consists mainly of songs that helped me cope during all of the depressive episodes of my life, most of which I am embarrassed of by now, because they serve as proof that I once needed them. My playlist makes me think about how at some point, I fell out of love with these songs because, in some small way, they had succeeded in saving me in the exact moments I needed them to, and now that I've used them up, they can no longer work in serving that purpose. But among the songs on my playlist, there are also some songs I cling to loving, that feel like songs that I must never stop loving.

I think that sometimes, we love, and we continue to have faith in the things we love, because the things that you love the most strongly are the things that will embarrass you the most deeply if you ever fall out of love with them.

The playlist for my funeral is 252 songs long now, and I feel like it's not done yet. I feel like it's still missing pieces, or that I haven't found the perfect single song that I love more than any of these other songs that would render my list obsolete. And I think I want to keep adding to it. And I think that means, that this is some sure sign, that I want to be alive.

Another conversation with another close friend who I also haven't spoken to now in years

...Oh.

Pieces

The more you grow as a person, the more homes you find, the more homes you make, the more homes you share. Each return to a home you once left becomes a realization that it takes up a smaller and smaller place among all the homes you now know. It's only natural to feel like you're being torn into pieces.

My grandfather's plant

When I was born, my parents were both graduate students. I was a little kid when my mom got her PhD and I remember going to her ceremony (I don't remember my dad's PhD ceremony, though I know he must have had one too, because he also has a PhD). It was in an enormous gymnasium—or maybe it just felt like a gymnasium to me at the time—and I remember sitting in the bleachers—again, I don't actually remember if they were bleachers or if this is just an extension of my imagining that the ceremony took place in a gym—with my grandparents, my brother, and my dad, and my dad turned to me and my brother and said, "When your mom's name gets called, I want you two to cheer as loud as you can for her." And when she got on stage to accept her degree, we stood up and cheered and made all the noise we could.

After the ceremony, after the bleachers in the gymnasium were put away—again, assuming we actually sat in bleachers and the ceremony actually took place in a gymnasium—we met my mom at the foot of the stage, where the organizers had started stacking the folding chairs and removing the Velcroed curtains around the edge of the stage and piling together all these long, tangly vines in these cheap little plastic planters that they had brought in for the purposes of making the gymnasium look prettier for the ceremony—again, if it was a gymnasium at all.

My grandfather said, "They are going to throw these plants away anyway, so why don't we take one of them to remember this day by?" and he didn't ask anyone and he just took one as we left.

That plant, that long, tangly vine, lived in my grandparents' house and it grew and grew and reached its way down the bookshelf it sat on top of, and across the top of the window frame next to it, and up around the light fixture hanging from the ceiling, growing in all directions, with the house holding it up, providing the structure it needed as it grew.

Even after my grandfather passed away, and the garden and all the vegetables in the backyard stopped growing, that one vine still grew, still stayed watered, still stayed taken care of, still survived.

And every time we visited grandma's house, it was still there, holding on to more and more of the house each time.

It felt like my grandfather, in a way, wasn't completely gone.

Sometimes, a plant is just a plant, but sometimes, caring for a plant feels like some way to do *something* when you don't know what else to do. Sometimes, caring for a plant feels like a way to remember someone, a way to, in some way, continue caring for them. Sometimes, you keep caring for the plant, and the plant keeps growing, discovering new corners to inhabit, new walls to climb.

Years later, my grandma moved out of that house and into a small apartment in a seniors' community. We visit her as much as we possibly can, but now I can't remember if the vine moved with her, too.

On remembering through others

From time to time, you will hear their voice in someone else's words. This is how they tell you, "I was part of the world and the world is still here."

Plants are already there, too

When I first moved to Cambridge, during a particularly depressive period of my life, I would look at the ground a lot. I started noticing and admiring the plants on the ground that I would walk past on my walks alone to school, to the store, to the movie theater where I would go watch movies by myself. One type of plant that I found particularly strange sat low to the soil, a bouquet of large leaves, clumped and repeated all around. Was someone planting these all over the place? Why did all the clumps seem like they were the exact same size? Why were there no smaller or larger clumps like them anywhere? And I started seeing this same plant everywhere I went, seemingly on every street (again, *Who was putting them everywhere?*). Noticing them made me feel more connected to my environment—like I was seeing some secret code that was showing me that every new place is made up of consistent pieces. (There is a part of me that finds this form of comfort in building codes for the same reason, because they necessitate that almost every unfamiliar building I walk into has something in common with a building that I may have called home at some point in my life.)

There is a tree in Cambridge that used to bloom in the springtime outside of my therapist's office. I say "used to" not because it doesn't bloom anymore, but because I don't know if it's still there. The tree may or may not still be there, but I am what the "used to" refers to: I'm what has gone. I don't see my therapist in person anymore. We talk over the phone now. But sometimes I see that same type of tree in different cities, in different countries. It makes me feel at peace. It reminds me that I once found a home where that tree grew, and so if that same tree can grow somewhere else, perhaps so can I.

And so now whenever I am in an unfamiliar place, it has become a coping mechanism for me to look for plants that I recognize from elsewhere, and to look for plants that I've never seen before anywhere else but that I can start recognizing as familiar when they show up again and again all over this unfamiliar place, making it more and more familiar in the process.

It's part of why I got so invested in caring for houseplants, too—so that I could start to spot the plants that I care about out in the world, in unfamiliar offices and shops and restaurants and buildings, or, at the very least, in unfamiliar plant stores that I will pop into when I am in unfamiliar cities.

This game of searching for and spotting and recognizing has made the anxiety of going to new places give way to something that feels a little bit more like excitement, because now I have the chance to be somewhere where all these plants I already know might be waiting to greet me.

Part 6: Goodbye, Again

Everything turned out fine; all I needed to do was live under constant and overwhelming stress and pressure forever

Something my therapist talks me through when I am anxious about highly stressful events happening is getting me to imagine what it will feel like *right after* that big scary stressful event is over. To give space to *what if it's a disaster* and *what if everything goes the absolute worst it could go* but to also give equal space to *well what if it goes okay* and even *well what if it goes well?*

And I say, sure, but this bad thing can happen and this bad thing can happen and this bad thing can happen.

And he says, "But what if it doesn't?"

And I say, "But what if it does?"

And he says, "Right . . . but what if it doesn't?"

Some plants were meant to die

I still get inordinately anxious when my plants show signs of stress: browning leaves, limp branches, overall sogginess. I worry too much and too intensely about them dying. And sometimes it feels utterly hopeless and that there is nothing I can do.

I think about a piece of advice, or perhaps just a piece of lament, that I was given from a plant shop owner who I was talking to about some plants that I bought (from a different plant shop than theirs) that had died under my care. They said that sometimes, plants are already doomed from the moment you bought them—they were already rotted, or they already had a disease, or the soil they were potted in was the wrong kind or the wrong pH level. They said that sometimes, when you bought them they were already dying and they just didn't show you that they were yet.

I ask, "But what about the plants that you take care of and that seem to be healthy for years before they one day die on you?" And the plant shop owner shrugs and says, "Sometimes it's not anything you did."

I don't know how true that is, but perhaps it doesn't need to be. Perhaps, just hearing someone say that to me is comfort enough.

Peperomia

The first houseplant I ever bought for myself as an adult was almost an accident. I had walked into a new plant store that just opened up near the building I just moved into, which meant we were both newcomers, and I saw that I was the only customer inside, and I felt so bad about leaving without buying anything that I picked out a small, very cute, very little plant with round, very plump, very matte green leaves that was on the display labeled, "Easy to care for."

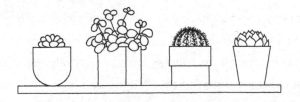

When I walked out of the store, into the cold, I grew immediately anxious because it had dawned on me that I was now solely responsible for keeping this plant alive. It had no one else to keep it alive but me.

I didn't know anything about how to care for a plant, but the plant store owner had said that this one was pretty hardy, that all I needed to do was water it a little bit a few times a week, and that it would survive in any type of light. I was immensely worried that I would somehow get this wrong (How much water is "a little bit"?! How many times a week is "a few"??), but after a few months of it not dying on me, I started to feel like I could handle taking care of it.

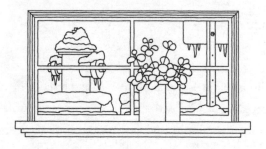

I found myself growing attached to it. For a while, it was the only living thing in my basement-level—sorry, *Garden-Level*—apartment aside from myself. And it helped keep me stable, in a way. I was deep inside a depressive year and having this little plant that I knew I had to water a few times a week was a gentle enough motivation for me to add some consistency in my life without adding too much pressure.

That summer, I had to go away, and I lent my plant to the one friend I had made in this city since moving here so they could take care of it while I was gone, which they then asked the person subletting their apartment to take care of, because they later found out they also had to go away for the summer. They assured me that their subletter was a good friend of theirs who would not let the plant die.

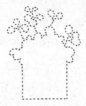

I was worried sick about my plant for the whole summer and I hoped that my worry was somehow helping it stay alive because there was nothing else I could do but worry. And after I got back at the end of the summer, and after my friend got back at the end of the summer, my friend brought my plant back to me and I saw that it had changed.

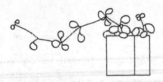

It thinned out, and was basically one long stem now that stretched heavily in one direction, reaching for where my friend's window was from its spot where it hadn't been moved all summer. But still, it was alive. And now it was back home. And I was grateful for that.

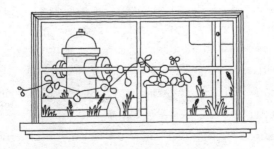

That fall, I started taking care of more plants because this plant had given me the confidence to do so, and when I started doing much more elaborate research on how to care for each of the new plants I had obtained, I realized that I didn't know what this little cute plant with the round plump leaves was even called. After some deep online investigation, I found out it was called a peperomia "hope" plant. And I like that in the first plant I ever cared for as an adult, I had brought into my life some hope.

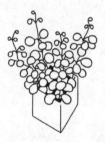

Years later, after the hope plant had grown bushy and filled out its little square pot with many limbs and many leaves, it slowly started to die, by the process of falling to pieces.

It was terrifying because it looked like it always did, green and plump and healthy, but when I brushed against one of its leaves, the leaf disconnected from its stalk immediately and fell.

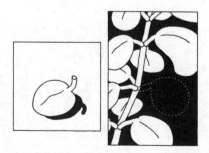

I tried not to panic and convinced myself that this was perhaps one of those naturally falling leaves that I might be able to propagate, so I set it aside to potentially grow roots.

I was careful not to touch the plant after that, hoping it was just this one leaf that fell, and that everything would be okay if I left it.

And a few days passed, and the leaf that fell off dried and shriveled up instead of growing roots.

A few more days passed, and I decided to touch another leaf on the plant, just to make sure that the leaf that *had* fallen was just an isolated incident, but then the new leaf I touched fell, too, and then the entire stalk collapsed into pieces of leaf and stem, separating at its joints, under my finger.

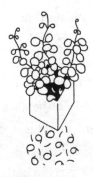

The plant at this point had grown into having four main stalks (now three because one of those stalks just collapsed), and I checked each of the remaining three stalks in the same way, just by tapping one of the leaves on each stalk, to see if that one collapsing stalk was an anomaly, but each of these three remaining stalks fell apart at the joints, too, leaves detaching, collapsing at my touch. I was left with a pile of pieces of a whole plant. It looked like my plant had become disassembled.

I didn't know what to do, so I saved every leaf and set each of them aside, in case any of them would grow roots so that I could propagate them.

 settings settings settings settings settings

At first, I was hopeful. I saw it as one plant becoming thirty round, plump leaves, potentially becoming thirty new plants. But every morning I would check on the leaves and every morning, a batch of them would be shriveled up.

ℰℰℰℰℰℰℰℰℰℰℰℰℰℰℰℰℰℰℰℰℰℰℰℰℰℰℰ

I held on to a belief that if even one of these leaves started growing roots, this would not be a complete tragedy. Over the next week, though, every single leaf dried out. Instead of just collapsing and dying the one time, my plant created thirty little pieces out of itself and divided its death into thirty little funerals.

After all the leaves died, I decided to keep the little square pot that my plant had grown in, as some way to remember that it once had grown in it. I didn't throw out the soil in the pot either, though I have less of a reason for why I kept that. It was because, I guess, hey, free soil.

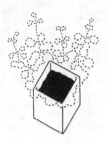

I pulled out the plant's roots from the soil, now that the roots had nothing to feed. Examining them, I saw there was no sign of root rot, so that couldn't have been the reason for my plant's demise. It was a mystery. I didn't know how to test if the soil became somehow toxic or too salty or too acidic or too basic or had become drained of its nutrients, so maybe one of those was the cause? But eventually I settled on believing that the cause of death was just that the plant had decided to give up and fall to pieces. That it was its time to go, and it had decided to wait to say goodbye until the next time I had greeted it with a touch of its leaves.

In my grief, I bought another plant—not the same kind, because I would never think of trying to *replace* my hope plant. And by chance, I had found a single, detached succulent leaf lying on top of this new plant's soil.

This detached leaf wasn't the same type of succulent as the plant I *had* bought, which had long, tubular leaves, whereas this leaf

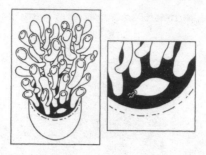

was bulbous and small, so it's a mystery what kind of succulent this leaf came from. But I noticed that the leaf had tiny, tiny tendrils of roots forming at its base, and I still had the empty little square pot of soil that my hope plant had collapsed in, so I set the new leaf onto the soil in that empty little square pot.

And I still didn't know if my hope plant had died because the soil was toxic or too salty or too acidic or too basic or had become drained of its nutrients, but the new leaf started to root in that same soil, which I took to be a good sign, at least.

And over time, with a little bit of watering a few times a week, a tiny, tiny sprout grew, with two tiny, fragile, thin leaves reaching up.

And now something else is growing, a new plant, in the same pot as my first plant.

Like some sort of rebirth.

To be happy is to be vulnerable

It's in the moments of happiness where I feel the most vulnerable to thoughts of sadness and of hopelessness. Because if happiness is here now, it means it's going to leave later, and after that comes the crash where I am aware that I no longer feel happy.

And sometimes it feels easier for me to avoid feeling happy—to kill it as soon as I start feeling it—to avoid these complications, and because if I avoid that happiness, the crash that follows it can be avoided, too.

It's hard for me to be happy because in the moment that I feel it, I tell myself that it's going to go away, that I know things are going to go back to feeling terrible, that it can't last, so it's a waste of my energy to be happy now.

But I am trying to tell myself more that happiness *has to be* temporary for it to exist. If it lasted forever, we wouldn't know to call it anything.

And maybe in recognizing that joy needs to be fleeting, instead of admonishing myself for celebrating something that I know is going to go away, maybe I can celebrate the feeling while I can, in the moments I feel it, before it disappears, because I know it will disappear, and because I don't know when that feeling will return, and so I may as well welcome it while it is still around.

Popcorn story

I don't think two people reaching into the same tub of popcorn at the same time is considered romantic. That's not romantic! That's just getting in the way of each other's popcorn.

Popcorn story (addendum)

Okay, okay, I guess what's romantic is when you are too shy to hold hands with somebody, and you graze their hand on the way to reaching for some popcorn in the giant bucket between you, and then, suddenly not knowing what to do, you for some reason decide that the best course of action is to plunge your entire hand into the giant bucket filled with popcorn.

They notice what you've done, then smile, then do the same thing. Then, gently, feeling their way through the popcorn, they reach out and take your hand in theirs, or you reach out and take their hand in yours, or you both do both at the same time. Then you watch the rest of the movie with your hands firmly holding each other's inside this bucket of popcorn, buttery and sweaty and salty.

After the movie ends, you don't want to stop holding hands, so you both carry this bucket of popcorn between the two of you as you leave the theater, with your hands still inside, still holding on to each other. You walk outside together, still holding hands in the popcorn in the bucket between you, until you get to the door of the place where one of you lives. And one of you asks if the other would like to do this again sometime, and the other responds that they would, and then one of you asks *Well, what should we do with this bucket?,* and then one of you decides to hold on to it as you both then let go of each other and take your hands out of the bucket and say good night, and goodbye, until you see each other again.

In order to continue holding hands, you bring the bucket of popcorn every time you see each other—to get ice cream, to other movies, to the park on the weekend. Eventually, the popcorn gets eaten (by you, by them, by the birds that pass by in the park), and so you are left just holding hands inside an empty bucket, sometimes bumping up against its greasy sides.

You bring this empty bucket to your place, to their place, so you can continue to hold hands in those places, too. Months later, you bring it into the place you decide to live in together. And this goes on for years. The bucket becomes so much a part of your lives that you barely notice it's even there.

Then, while holding hands in the bucket over breakfast one morning, one of you speaks up, and says, "Why do we still hold hands in this bucket? It just keeps making our hands buttery." And you both agree to get rid of the bucket, and then only your hands remain, holding each other, popcorn and butter and bucket and salt no longer necessary.

Something that Elissa told me once that I repeat to myself every day

You have your entire life to worry about the rest of your life. Just get through today. Don't tell yourself "don't worry," but just . . . worry smaller.

Visiting happiness

If happiness visits, let yourself let it in.

Don't judge it, don't give it a side eye. It's not trying to trick you.
Trust that it's here to see you.

It comes too rarely for you to ask yourself if you deserve it.

Just sit next to it for as long as it sits next to you. You can at least let yourself do that.

Then, let it join the other happinesses that may be visiting you in that same moment.

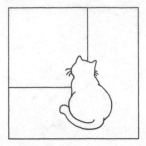

And when it wants to leave, let it leave. You can't force it to stay. It's going to leave regardless.

And even though this specific happiness might not come back, know that it has to leave for it to visit you again.

Bird window

A friend posted a photo of a bird the other day. It was a round, plump, unassuming, dark-brown bird, sitting on the windowsill outside a window. After a few days, they posted another photo of the same bird sitting outside the same window. Then, a few more days after that, another photo of the same bird at the same window, only this time, my friend had noted that the bird was facing a different direction than in the previous photos. "Who is that!" I eventually had to ask. They told me it was their new friend: The bird has been sitting outside the same window of the library for the last three weeks.

Because of the bird, that corner of the library, where the window is, where the bird sits on the other side of, has become my friend's favorite place to read. Every time they're there, the bird is there, too.

"Maybe it also wants to read," I say, "but it isn't allowed inside."

"You should hold a book up to the window and see if it stays or flies away," I joke after they don't respond.

Really, what I find myself wondering is if it will still be my friend's favorite place to read after the bird stops coming.

Visiting sadness

I am always sad when I think about happinesses leaving, but I have started to understand that sadnesses can leave, too.

I have been trying lately to welcome sadness like a bird that's come to perch on a branch nearby for a moment.

I try to just sit quietly and observe its details, to try to understand what is unique and special and different about this bird, to try to take note of what features I can use to identify it before it flies away.

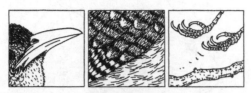

I find a little bit of happiness— or maybe, at least, comfort— in observing these sadnesses, and in identifying them with enough resolution that I am able to recognize them when they approach.

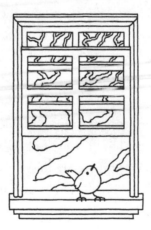

And when they approach, I let them in, to join all the other sadnesses visiting me at the moment.

I have started to let sadnesses visit whenever they come, because I know that trying to keep them out will just cause them to find another, more aggressive way in.

And when they visit, I try to sit with them, and understand the different nuances between these visitors, to take stock of them and note how each of them makes me feel. It helps me realize that they are not all the same—that sadness is not just one consistently gray, same-feeling blob—but that there are different kinds of sadnesses, some more common, some more rare. And when they visit, I have started to find some form of small excitement in the fact that these are the only chances I get to feel them and to observe their details firsthand. It becomes a form of birdwatching, in a way.

And when I take the time to observe how I feel when each of them is around, I can identify when I don't feel those ways any longer.

That means they have gone, at least for a moment.

And after doing this for long enough, I have submitted to the fact (or the feeling, perhaps), that each of these specific sadnesses is going to return, likely again and again over the course of my entire life.

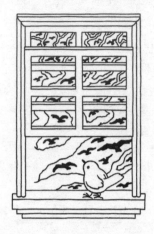

But for each sadness to return, it first has to leave.

Your last 15 minutes before the end of the world, ranked from worst to best

15.   Minute fifteen: Seeing for the first time an alert that the world will end in fifteen minutes. The feeling of a lurching stomach and a sweating that will not stop. Waiting for a breathing that will not start.

14.   Minute four: Realizing, fully without hope, how truly little time you have left. Four minutes may be enough time, on average, to listen to a favorite song of yours, in full, one final time. But, perhaps, not enough time to properly deliberate among all the options for what song that should be, to make a fully thought-out choice on which one you want to hear, and then have enough time left to play it all the way through. Not knowing what else to do, you decide to go with silence, and move your furniture around so that you can sit and look directly out the window, and up at the sun, and, at least, feel the daylight flooding in.

13.   Minute eleven: Finding out the reason why the world is ending, confirming that yes, the world will end, that all this news is real, and being filled with a rage and a hopelessness and a complete and utter lack of surprise, a feeling of, *oh, well of course this is how it's all going to end, of course it is, of course.*

12.   Minute seven: Listening too long to the ringing as you try to FaceTime your mom.

11.   Minute ten: The deep anxiety in realizing that five minutes have already passed since you found out that the world was going to end, and that you would do anything to get those five minutes back.

10.   Minute five: Being on a group FaceTime with your entire family, being grateful that at least, in this small way, you are together, even though you are not saying anything at all, even though you are all just crying, and you are just watching your mom take screenshot after screenshot of her own screen, even though there is no reason to save any more screenshots any longer. Every few seconds, she will accidentally fail to press the lock button and the volume button at the exact same time, and her video will go dark, and your heart plummets, but then you hear her voice saying that she just locked her screen by accident, and her face will appear again. You think about getting upset at her for doing this, to tell her to just be present, but then you say nothing, and start taking screenshots, too. For what seems like forever, you are all just taking screenshots, saying nothing in a quiet agreement, just saving screenshots of each other knowing that they won't matter but not knowing

what else to do—and then your call gets disconnected. You try to call back, and you connect, but the video is a useless pixelated blur. The audio is choppy. But through it, you can still tell your mom is taking screenshots of the call. Then, the call gets disconnected again, and this time, you can't call back. You can't get any signal. You check your data and it's gone. The network has been disconnected, or maybe overloaded. Either way, it's the same outcome to you.

9.   Minute thirteen: Opening your phone to check the news and feeling the brief, final moment of uncertainty and doubt you will ever feel. The last time you will ever think, *this can't be real, can it?* with any amount of trust in your own disbelief.

8.   Minute nine: Crying, not in fear, but as a way to distract yourself from the fear.

7.   Minute eight: The clarity of feeling everything you thought you cared about sloughing off you, slipping away, leaving you dizzy, disoriented, with a feeling of lightness. There is so little that truly matters, isn't there? But what remains is real, and now, at least, you can live the rest of your life knowing with certainty that what remains is what is truly important to you.

6.   Minute six: "Hey, are you okay?" "Yeah. I don't know. Yes. Are you?" "We love you." "Is dad okay?" "I'm okay." "Is Chris okay?" "We are trying to call him." "He's not answering." "No." "Okay. I love you." "We love you." "Wait, he's calling, let me loop him in." "Hey I'm scared, I tried to reach you." "We're here." "I love you." "I love you." "I love you." "I love you." "I love you." "I love you." "I love you."

5.   Minute three: Realizing the reason she took those screen-shots was because she will be looking at those as the world ends. Then, being overwhelmed with gratitude, you take out your phone and look at your own screenshots. You wish you had more photos of them, but at least you have these. Then, crying again, not in fear, but as a way to con-nect yourself to love, knowing that the ones you love are crying, too.

4.   Minute fourteen: Realizing that you are, through some small—or quite large—miracle, finding all of this out while sitting in the same room as the person you love, who you have committed to loving, who you have chosen to spend the rest of your life with, and realizing, for better or for worse, this is it.

3.   Minute two: Turning off your phone, looking at the person you love, and declaring the things that matter most to you.

2.   Minute one: Reaching a state of calm and accepting that all that you've done with your time on earth is enough, be-cause it must be enough, because it is all that it will ever be.

1.   Minute twelve: Laughing at a good meme about the end of the world you saw online while you were in the middle of figuring out what was going on.

The tree outside my therapist's office

I am visiting Cambridge for a couple days. I used to live here, and I do not anymore.

I am standing in front of the tree that used to bloom in the spring outside of my therapist's office. It is still here. Still standing, too.

I used to walk past this tree on the way to my therapist every week and it used to bring me joy and calm. I would think, *You're still here, and I'm still here. That makes two of us, okay?*

And in the winters when I would walk by it, it would stand, barren. In the winters, I'd be so convinced of its stillness that I would be overwhelmed with the thought, *It would be so easy for you, and for every tree, to just stay as you are and never grow leaves ever again. What's stopping you from just stopping completely?*

And today, in the course of my visiting, I found myself wondering about this tree, and I found myself taking a detour through the area just to see if this tree was still here, and it brings me immense joy and relief to see that the tree still is, even as other things I remember about this place are not.

And today just happens to be a day in the spring, so the tree is covered in its own flowers, blooming as if to say, *Don't worry about me. I'm just doing tree stuff. Like always. Worry about yourself, maybe. Stop moving around so much, maybe. It's making me tired. Just sit still in the sun for a couple weeks. Trust me, it'll feel nice.*

I believe that the things you notice—that you love, that make you pause—make up who you are. And so it feels, in a way, like those things are a part of you, even though they are outside of you. Which makes me wonder if it would be more accurate to say, perhaps, that a piece of you is kept alive by a part of them.

I wonder how many other people think about this tree, or remember it when they think about this street, or this neighborhood, or this city. I wonder how many other people stood among its low branches and giant flowers in the spring and felt surrounded by it and thought for just a moment, *Nothing else matters. I am surrounded by flowers blooming on the branches of a tree in the spring and I am in the sun and everything will be fine.*

And of course everything will not be fine. But I believe that what defines us, in part, are the things we draw ourselves to that make us believe that they might, for a brief moment, be okay.

They say that you are alive for as long as someone remembers something about you. I would like to believe that a home remembers you for as long as one thing you remember of it is still there.

Someone else's room

One of the first places I lived alone in was a tiny shoebox studio unit on the twelfth floor of an apartment building. The bed was in the kitchen and the kitchen was along the back wall of the bedroom because it was all one single room.

One night, I got off the elevator on the floor of my apartment and felt like something had changed, even though the hallway looked exactly the same as it always had.

But still, this hallway that I'd walked down every day felt different, and I couldn't explain why until I got to my apartment.

My key didn't turn in the lock, but as an ordinary, every-day reflex, I moved to open my door anyway, and I found that it opened.

When I stepped in, I saw a room that had the exact same walls as mine, the exact same outer shell, but it was filled with different stuff. Everything was wrong. I didn't recognize the shapes that filled it. This was someone else's home.

I immediately stepped out and closed the door and backed away. For a split second, I felt confused. This is where my apartment should be. Then I looked at the metal numbers on the door and I realized that this apartment was in the same place as my apartment was, only on a different floor. I was not on the floor of my apartment at all. I had somehow hit the wrong button on the elevator without noticing and had gotten off on the floor below mine. And this was why the hallway, and the walk leading to my unit, felt uncanny.

As soon as I realized this, I hurried back to the elevator, afraid that there was someone in the unit I had just intruded on, though I stepped out and closed the door so quickly that I hadn't seen if there was. As I walked back up the hallway, I felt this intense weight all around me, as if I was seeing a hallway I was never meant to see—and that if I didn't get out of here fast enough, I would somehow get trapped here and would never be able to leave.

The elevator took forever to come and I feared that I was already too late—that this hallway had already felt my presence and this was the end and I would never be seen again.

But the elevator doors opened, and I stepped into it, and I looked very carefully at the buttons and made sure to press the correct floor number this time, and then I held my breath until the elevator doors opened on my actual floor.

The hallway looked exactly the same but felt familiar now and I rushed to my actual apartment with my key clutched tightly in my hand.

The key turned in the lock this time and I unlocked my door without looking behind me, and then I went inside, and then I closed my door, and then I locked it.

Even in the dark, the shadows in this room were ones that I recognized, and I breathed a sigh of relief. I was home.

Home, then, I suppose, is simply in the ways you take a strange space and make it feel familiar. Sometimes that means putting your stuff in it. Sometimes that just means putting yourself in it and giving it time.

———

Every winter, I go back to visit the house I grew up in.

I stand in my old bedroom and try to remember what it felt like to be a younger me living here, instead of being a visitor to the memory of what "here" even is. Here, all my stuff has stayed exactly the same as I remember from that time. It is frozen—a memorial, in a way, to some past version of me who is gone now, who I no longer am.

And it doesn't feel like home anymore. Standing in my old bedroom feels uncanny, just a little bit like standing in the apartment below mine. Only instead of having stepped into a hallway on the wrong floor, I am standing in my home in the wrong time.

I suppose sometimes the things in the room don't need to be different for a place to feel unfamiliar.

Sometimes you are the thing that has changed.

Goodbye, again

Every goodbye after our first should remind us that we've done this before.

Instead of *Goodbye*, I'd like to start saying *Goodbye, again*.

See you later cannot be promised, but *Goodbye, again* reminds us that we've done this before.

And after the last time, at least, we both came back.

AFTERWORD: *A small goodbye*

I didn't want working on this book to end. I enjoyed having this long, ongoing project because it gave me something I could always be working on. It allowed me to consider every stray thought I had as a potential contribution to the project, and even in considering its potential, even if that stray thought turned out to be nothing, I was still working because I was examining it. Since the task of making this book was to reflect, I found a comfort in knowing that every free moment I had was one when I could be working, somehow, in some way, by thinking, by examining, by considering whatever came by for me to consider. Even if I was not actively focusing on the project, or thinking about the project, I felt like I was still working on it, because I was gathering experience for things I could think about later and things I could potentially write about. Or, I was gathering rest, I was saving up time and energy so I could work on this again after. I enjoyed having an excuse to rest, because it was in the form of *it is contributing to my work*, in the form of *it is productive to rest so I can be more productive after I rest*, and I fear that now that this is over, I won't have that excuse anymore either.

I have enjoyed spending the last three years or so of my life examining and scrutinizing every thought that passed me by, hoping it might be something, and marking it down, and now that this book is done, I'm afraid I will not do that anymore because I will have no more reason to. I have enjoyed this period of time because it has allowed me to mean something. I feel that it has justified my time on this earth.

But maybe now this means that I can enjoy allowing a thought to just be a thought without it having to mean anything more than being a fleeting thought, without it having to be part of any project, without it having to be work. Maybe now, I can rest just for the sake of resting, without feeling like I need to have a reason to do so. Maybe after this, nothing can come next for a while, and that nothing will be welcomed.

I believe that any creative project is an archive, or a time capsule, some marking down of some sense of who you are, or were, at the specific moments in time that you were making it.

This book, I think, served as a way to put some part of myself into it and to take that part of myself out of me, in order to clear space in me to grow into something new, something changed. And afterward, I suppose, I will change and grow and change and grow again until I become some next version of myself who I am compelled to find a reason to archive again. Or maybe, I will grow into some version of me who is no longer compelled to archive myself at all, who doesn't need to turn every moment of myself into work. And wouldn't that be nice.

Maybe the lag time between when you make something and

when people see it is important, as it gives you enough time to mourn who you have preserved away before everyone else sees who that is for the first time.

I don't know that the me who is writing this right now will ever know for sure. Because by the time you read this book, the person who made it will be gone.

ACKNOWLEDGMENTS

Writing is a lonely act that summons all the people who have shaped you. You conjure them up to sit with you as you write so they can inform and shape your work. Writing is, then, to surround yourself with ghosts. Perhaps that makes it even lonelier, knowing that all the people whose memories appear are not actually with you at the time of the writing, but I try to hold on to the work as long as I can as a way to keep the memories of those people present when the people themselves are far away.

This is a way for me to feel like I am connected to them, even though they may never know this. I used to feel like that was enough, and I used to hope that somehow, when I was thinking about them, when I was writing and conjuring them, that they would somehow feel it, that they would somehow be thinking of me and feel connected to me too without me doing any of the actual work of reaching out. And I think my hoping that that was connection enough made me feel lonelier.

Some of these people who I conjure this way are no longer

here, so this feels like the only way I can be in conversation with them now, and that feels like enough, because it has to be.

But for those of them who are still around, I am trying now—instead of conjuring some idealized or projected memory of them—to just reach out and say hello to the living, real person. It turns out that letting someone know you are thinking about them is, on all counts, a much clearer way to let them know that you are thinking about them.

I have found comfort in knowing that I can live with a memory of someone for as long as I am around to remember them, but while the actual person that memory comes from is still here to say hello to, I am trying to say hello to them more, before I can no longer do that. And I feel lucky enough that, when I need these people, they continue to be here for me.

It feels impossible to capture my immense gratitude for all the people who have been and are in my life, because how can you capture the wholeness of all the lives that have been a part of yours, and that you have been a part of? So I am hoping these notes of thanks can be enough, in the place of knowing that no amount of acknowledgement can be enough to express my deepest gratitude.

———

Mary Gaule, my editor, who took this book on and saw it through to the end: I am indebted to your endless patience, insight, taste, wisdom, encouragement, and generosity. I couldn't have done this without you, and I'm grateful for your kindness and understanding through all of this.

In the years that this book existed as an idea and as notes

and drafts and sketches and more ideas, two other editors believed in it, too. Eric Meyers, who I remain forever grateful to for being the first person who I learned to make books with; and Stephanie Hitchcock, for helping me shape this one when it was more than two hundred scattered notes in my notes app, and for the most generous gift of suggesting the title, which oriented the entire book and made it what it became.

Jamie Kerner made the design of this book beautiful— thank you for putting up with all my endless notes and ideas, and for having all the patience and kindness and expertise to make this book look absolutely stunning. Stacey Fischkelta, for coordinating and making the production of this book all come together perfectly.

Heather Drucker, Megan Looney, Lisa Erickson, Iris McElroy, Beth Hicks, Dori Carlson, Amy Baker, and everyone at Harper Perennial: you are the best team to work with.

Thank you to my draft-readers, my dear and trusted friends whose notes shaped this book and whose friendships have shaped me. Reading your generous and honest thoughts and reactions to the drafts I sent you made me feel like we were in the same room together, which I hope we can be soon: Eve Ewing, Karen Chee, Clint Smith, Megan Amram, Mahdi Sabbagh, Maya Quetzali, and Chiara Wiik.

Friends and mentors who inspire and influence me: Raphael Bob-Waksberg, Steven Yeun, Lin-Manuel Miranda, Sarah Kay, Kevin Vidal, Danny Vidal, Zach Veach, Elena Baranes, Mun Hee Lee, Hiba Bhatty, Rozette Rago, Samantha Frank, Chaewon Ahn, Tony Vanky, Carina Cautillo, Amanda Bell, Ryan Alafriz, Jon Hoss, Heather Nguyen, Suzy Shinn,

Victoria Dawe, Dylan Marron, Meera Lee Patel, Mary H. K. Choi, Fatimah Asghar, the entire BEOTIS crew of writers and poets, Ben Schwartz, Lisa Hanawalt, Steve Cohen, Noel Bright, Hiro Murai, Andrew Jay Cohen, Demi Adejuyigbe, Hrishikesh and Lindsey Hirway, Kevin Porter, Sonny Lee, Shauna McGarry, Rachel Kaplan, Alison Tafel, Amy Schwartz, Joanna Calo, Elijah Aron, Minhal Baig, Peter Knight, Nick Adams, Mehar Sethi, Joe Lawson, Karen Joseph Adcock, Lorraine DeGraffenreidt, Chikodili Agwuna, and the entire *BoJack* season six writers room and team, from whom I have learned so much.

All the people and places named and unnamed in the book, for sharing with me all the experiences and memories that gave me a life to write about.

For the people I have lost in the last three years, who can now only exist in memory.

The Asian Students' Alliance at Vassar was the first group to whom I read what became the essay "Moving," back when it was just a floating idea and before an idea of this book even existed. I would like to express my deepest appreciation to all the Asian American student groups that I have been invited to speak with: you make me feel instantly part of a community and you give me a deep sense of hope and joy.

My therapist, Christer, who has helped me understand myself and grow in ways that I am incredibly proud of.

My team, for building with me a life where I get to invest in my creative work: Daniel Greenberg and Tim Wojcik at LGR Literary, Luke Maxwell and Luke Dillon at 3 Arts, Tabia Yapp and the entire team at BEOTIS, my entire team at UTA, and Brittany Gilpin. Thank you, thank you.

Ornella and Nick and Daniele, for your endless support and encouragement and for treating me as if I have always been family.

Lao Lao (Meifeng Zhang), Lao Ye (Keyi Feng), Ye Ye (Jiajun Sun), Nai Nai (Junxiu Chen), Nonna Santina, and Nonna Dora: I am thinking of you all the time.

My parents and my brother, for inspiring the heart of this book, and for shaping who I am and who I will become, and for, during my entire life, believing in and encouraging and supporting and loving me and my writing and my drawing and my entire creative existence. And for being so excited and proud, after I was so afraid of what you'd think, to see our lives written about in this book. I love you. Chris, for reading all this and asking, "How did you even remember any of this?" and for being the first person whose laugh I hear in my head whenever I realize something I think of might be worth writing down. And for the endless notes I will continue to get from the three of you on this book even after it has been published and is long past the point of being able to be edited.

Elissa, for choosing to share your life with me. When I had no idea what I was supposed to do with all of this, you were the one who believed in me, as you always do, and you said to me, "I think this should be the next book." For being the first and last person to hear about every idea and to read every draft and to see every sketch and to tell me which of the seemingly endless options is the one you like the most; for your endless advice and feedback; for telling me what is working and what doesn't make sense; and for telling me when to stop drawing because I'm at the point I'm just changing things for the sake of not wanting to be done with them. For putting up with all my sleepless nights and deadline days and for your limitless partnership and support and love and patience and intelligence and wisdom. In short, for everything. You are the reason I can do what I do. It is my greatest joy to share my life with you. I love you.

And finally, thank you to you, reading this, for allowing this version of me to be alive in your head for a little while. I really like being alive, so thank you.

ABOUT THE AUTHOR

JONNY SUN is the bestselling author and illustrator of *everyone's a aliebn when ur a aliebn too* and the illustrator of *Gmorning, Gnight!* by Lin-Manuel Miranda. He was a writer for the Emmy-nominated sixth season of the Netflix Original Series *BoJack Horseman*. His work has appeared in *The New Yorker* and *McSweeney's*. *Time* magazine named him one of the 25 Most Influential People on the Internet, and his TED Talk on loneliness has been viewed online more than 3.5 million times. As a doctoral candidate at MIT and a creative researcher at the Harvard metaLAB, he studies virtual place and online community. He received his master's degree in architecture from Yale and his bachelor's degree in engineering from the University of Toronto.

ABOUT THE TYPE

The text of *Goodbye, Again* is set in a typeface called Granjon, which is an old-style serif typeface designed by George W. Jones in 1928, based on the Garamond typeface. As there were several Garamond revivals on the market at the time, Jones named his type after Robert Granjon, whose italic design was commonly paired with the roman Garamond design. Notably, *Mastering the Art of French Cooking*, by Julia Child, Simone Beck, and Louisette Bertholle, is set in the Granjon typeface.

The cover of *Goodbye, Again* is set in a typeface called Bodoni Seventytwo Oldstyle, which is a digital revival of the modern serif typeface originally designed by Giambattista Bodoni in the late eighteenth century. The original Bodoni typeface followed the ideas of the Baskerville typeface to a more extreme conclusion and is known for its extreme vertical stress, fine hairlines contrasted by bold main strokes, and very subtle, almost nonexistent bracketing of sharply defined hairline serifs. Bodoni Seventytwo Oldstyle was designed for display in 1994 by Janice Fishman, Holly Goldsmith, Jim Parkinson, and Sumner Stone, who sought to design a revival that reflected the subtleties of Bodoni's original work.